Ingres

By Jessica Findley

First Edition

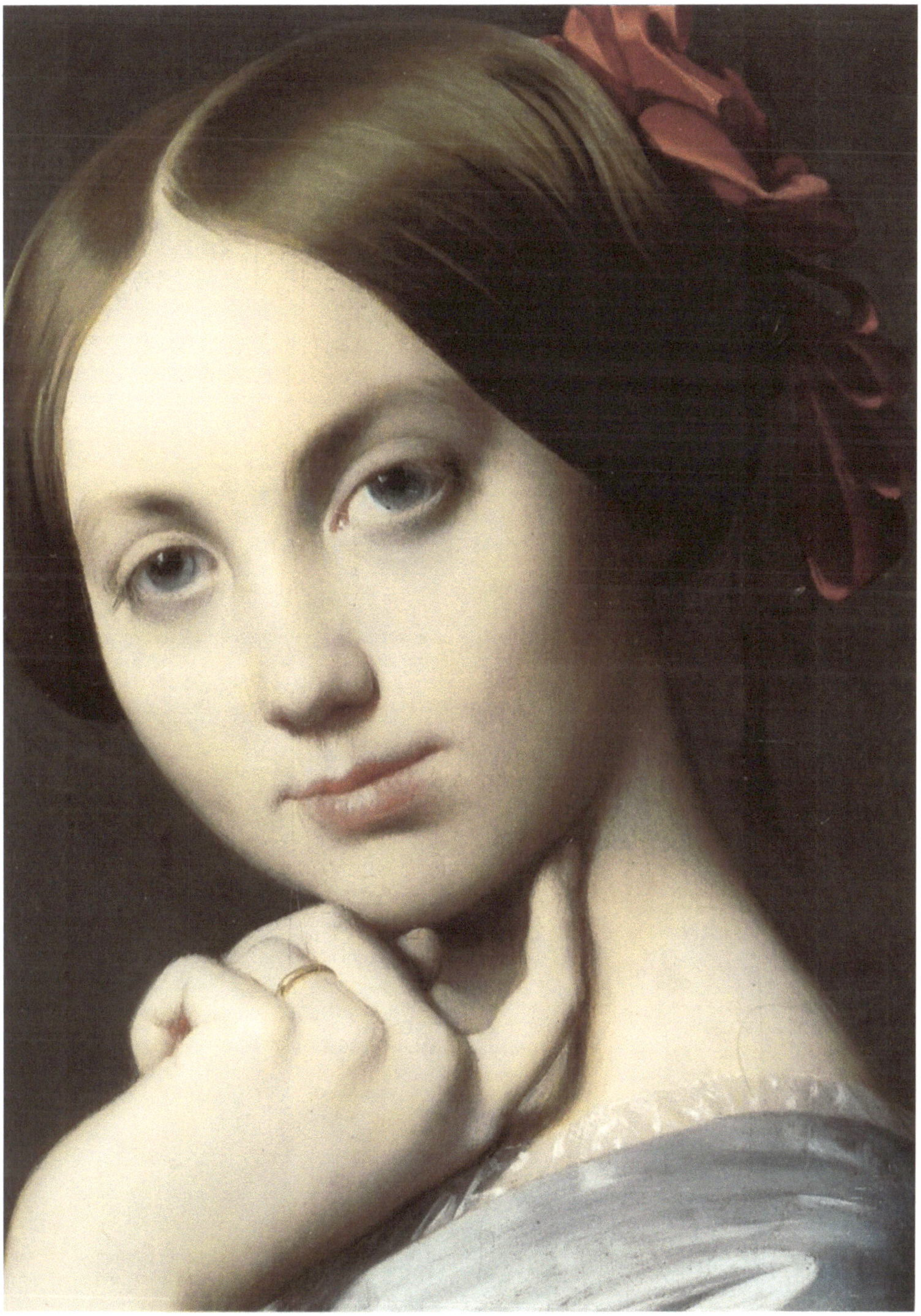

Detailed Masterpieces in Color

Foreword

Jean-Auguste-Dominique Ingres (1780 –1867) was a French Neoclassical painter. Although he considered himself to be a painter of history in the tradition of Nicolas Poussin and Jacques-Louis David, by the end of his life it was Ingres's portraits, both painted and drawn, that were recognized as his greatest legacy.

A man profoundly respectful of the past, he assumed the role of a guardian of academic orthodoxy against the ascendant Romantic style represented by his nemesis Eugène Delacroix. His exemplars, he once explained, were "the great masters which flourished in that century of glorious memory when Raphael set the eternal and incontestable bounds of the sublime in art ... I am thus a conservator of good doctrine, and not an innovator." Nevertheless, modern opinion has tended to regard Ingres and the other Neoclassicists of his era as embodying the Romantic spirit of his time, while his expressive distortions of form and space make him an important precursor of modern art.

Ingres is the son of a minor painter and sculptor, Jean-Marie-Joseph Ingres (1755-1814). After an early academic training in the Toulouse Academy he went to Paris in 1796 and was a fellow student of Gros in David's studio. He won the Prix de Rome in 1801, but owing to the state of France's economy he was not awarded the usual stay in Rome until 1807. In the interval he produced his first portraits. These fall into two categories: portraits of himself and his friends, conceived in a Romantic spirit (Self-portrait, 1804), and portraits of well-to-do clients characterized by purity of line and enamel-like colouring. These early portraits are notable for their calligraphic line and expressive contour, which had a sensuous beauty of its own beyond its function to contain and delineate form. It was a feature that formed the essential basis of Ingres's painting throughout his life.

During his first years in Rome he continued to execute portraits and began to paint bathers, a theme which was to become one of his favourites. He remained in Rome when his four-year scholarship ended, earning his living principally by pencil portraits of members of the French colony. But he also received more substantial commissions, including two decorative paintings for Napoleon's palace in Rome. In 1820 he moved from Rome to Florence, where he remained for 4 years, working mainly on his Raphaelesque Vow of Louis XIII, commissioned for the cathedral of Montauban.

Ingres's work had often been severely criticized in Paris because of its 'Gothic' distortions, and when he accompanied this painting to the Salon of 1824 he was surprised to find it acclaimed and himself set up as the leader of the academic opposition to the new Romanticism. Ingres stayed in Paris for the next ten years and received the official success and honours he had always craved. During this period he devoted much of his time to executing two large works: The Apotheosis of Homer, for a ceiling in the Louvre, and The Martyrdom of St Symphorian (1834) for the cathedral of Autun. When the latter painting was badly received, however, he accepted the Directorship of the French School in Rome, a post he retained for 7 years. He was a model administrator and teacher, greatly improving the school's facilities, but he produced few major works in this period.

In 1841 he returned to France, once again acclaimed as the champion of traditional values. He was heartbroken when his wife died in 1849, but he made a happy second marriage in 1852, and he continued working with great energy into his 80s. One of his acknowledged masterpieces, the extraordinarily sensuous Turkish Bath dates from the last years of his life. At his death he left a huge bequest of his work (several paintings and more than 4,000 drawings) to his home town of Montauban.

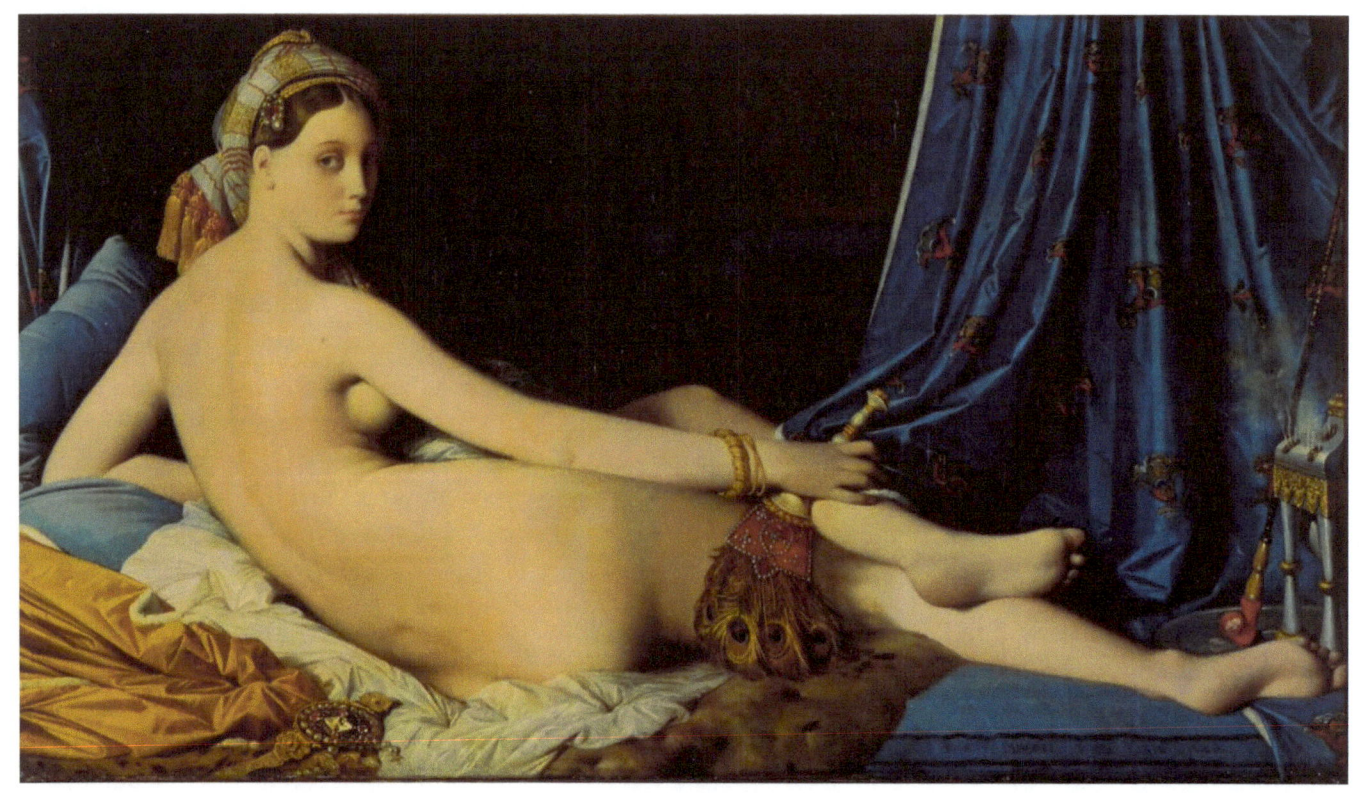

The Grande Odalisque

1814, oil on canvas

The effects in Ingres' paintings largely depend on drawing and linearity, but he also used colour to supremely calculated effect. The cold turquoise of the silk curtain with its decoration of red flowers intensified the warm flesh tone of the Grande Odalisque. This nude was painted in 1814 for Napoleon's sister, Queen Caroline Murat. Unlike the realism of Goya's Maja, Ingres' nude is hardly intimate, the eroticism here emerging slowly from the reserve and the questioning, assessing glance of the naked woman. This is a tradition that goes back to Giorgione and Titian, but Ingres has painted a living woman and not an allegory of Venus. Nevertheless, the realistic intimacy is lessened by setting the scene in the distant world of the Orient.

For many in the West, the idea of the harem with its available or exploited women trapped in their own closed world was as much proof of the fallen or primitive state of the East as was its supposed savagery. But it was also infinitely titillating. Ingres's picture is more than this, however. A sense of loss was inevitably embodied in French perceptions of the East after their defeat in Egypt, and it was perhaps because it sublimated unattainable desires that the theme of the Oriental nude, bather or harem girl gained such a haunting appeal. Ingres is remarkable for combining a frank allure with a chilling perfection of flesh. He had picked up his discreet hints of the harem — a turban here, a fan there — from Oriental artefacts and miniatures in the collections of Gros and Denon. They serve to locate his nude, who otherwise could really belong anywhere, in a sensuous Orient of the imagination.

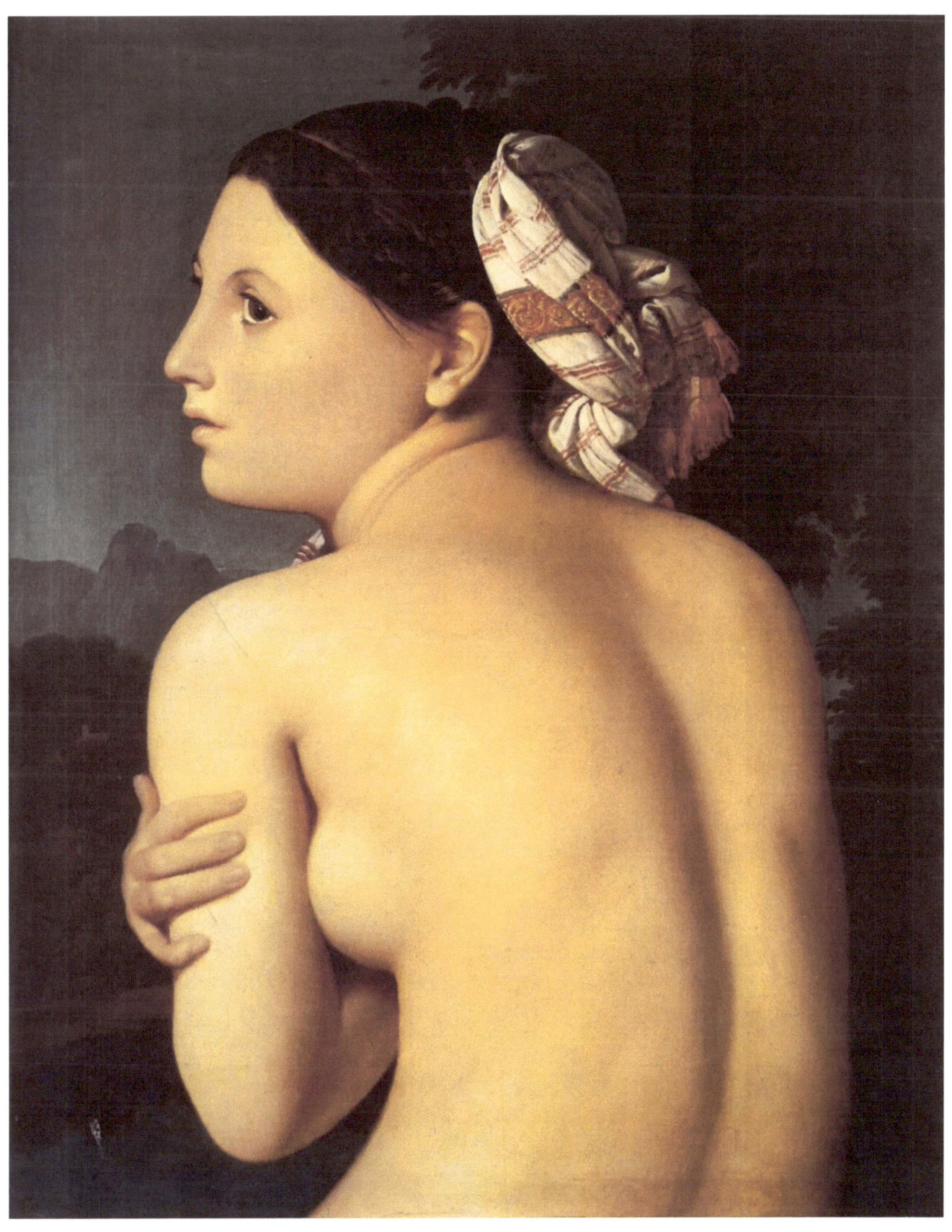

Half-figure of a Bather

1807, oil on canvas

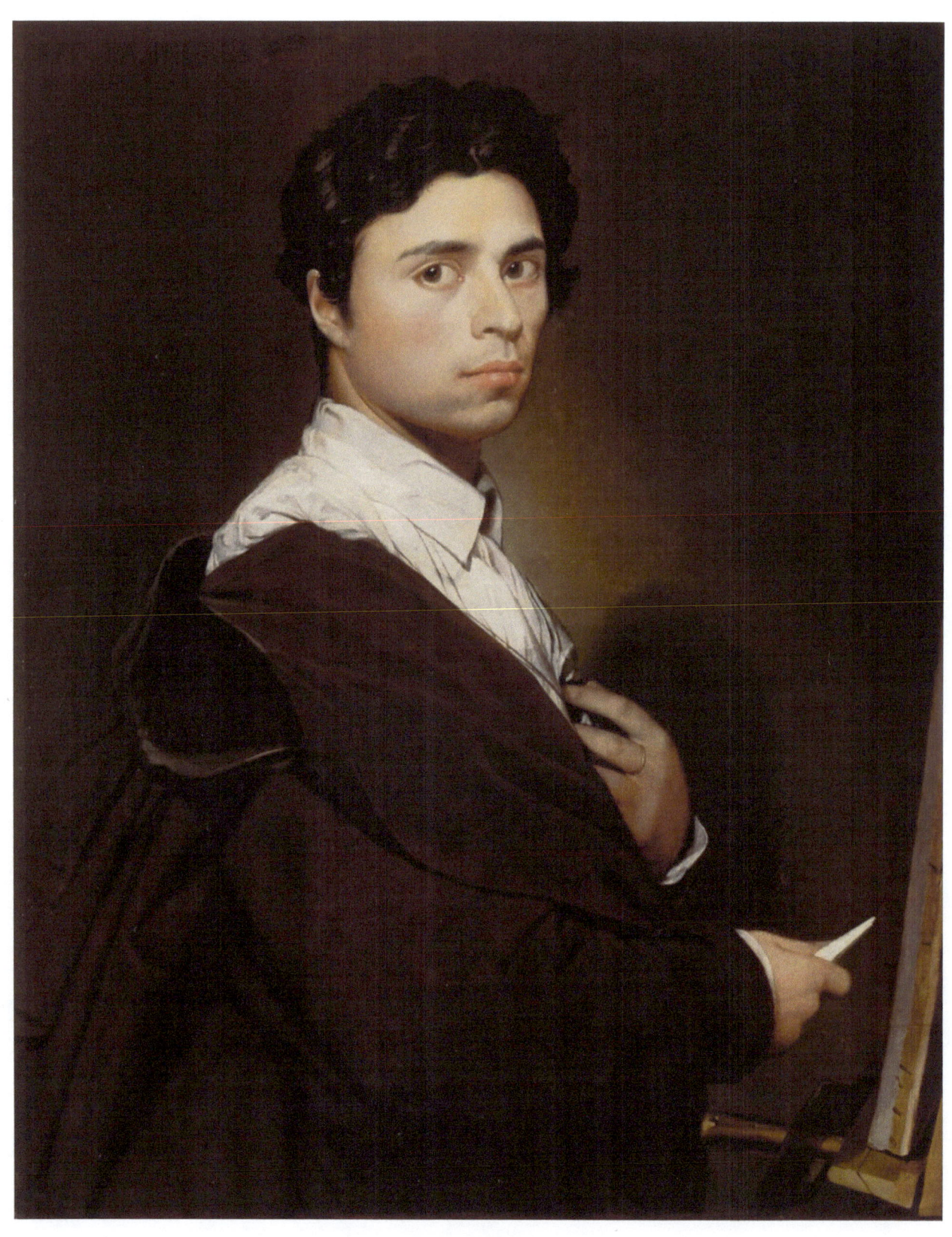

Self-Portrait at the Age of 24

1804, oil on canvas

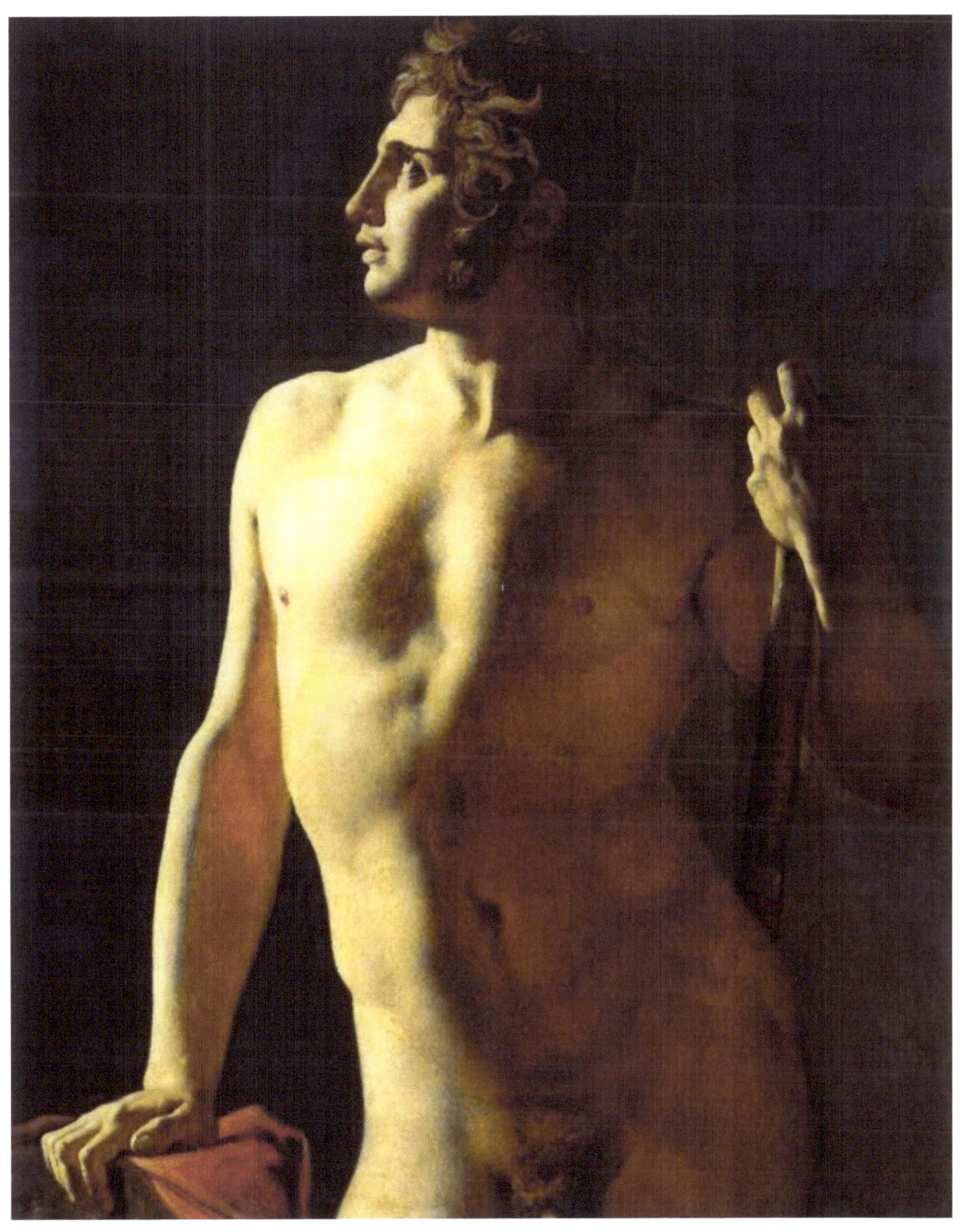

Male Torso

1800, oil on canvas

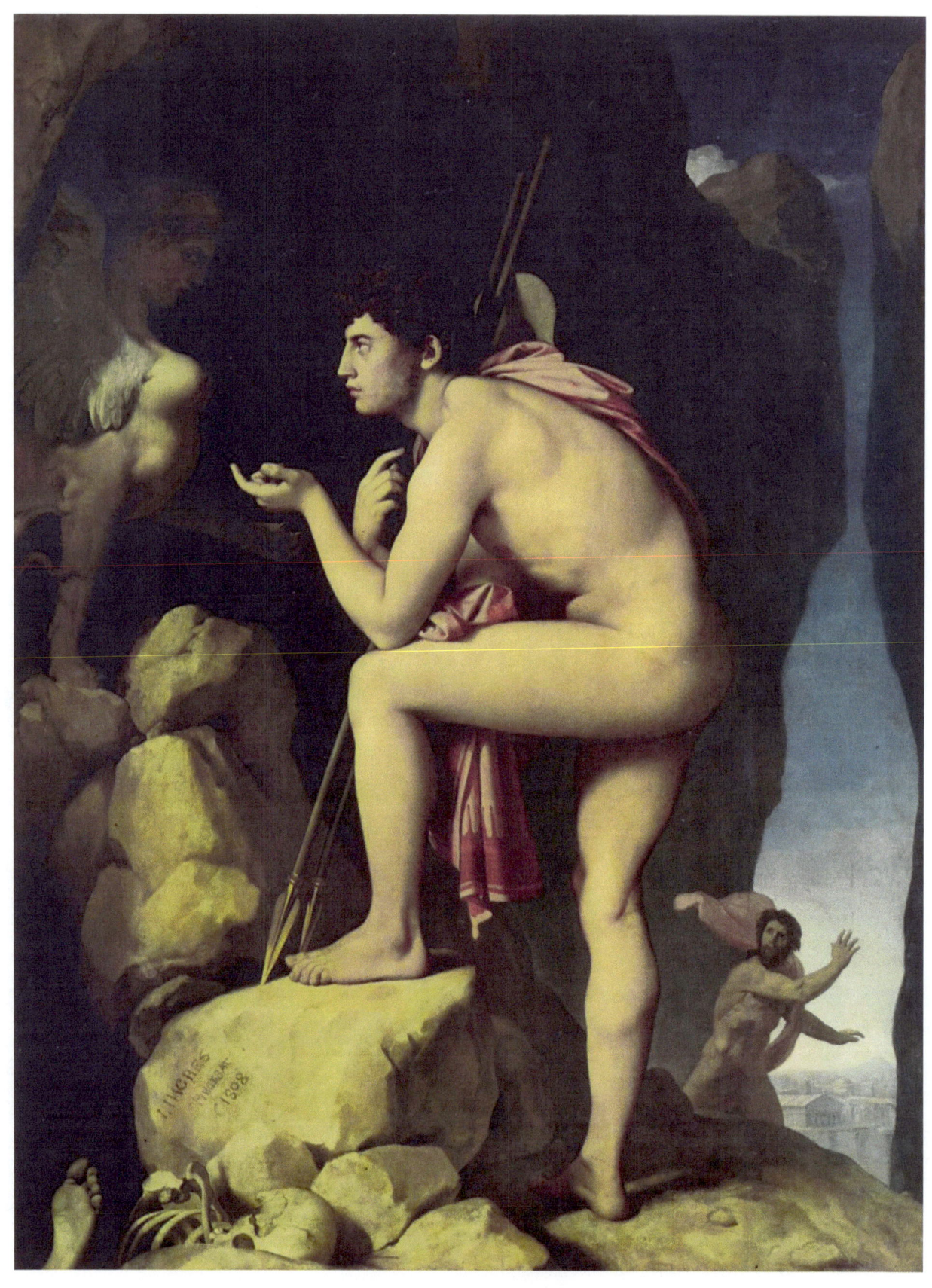

Oedipus and the Sphinx

1808-1825, oil on canvas

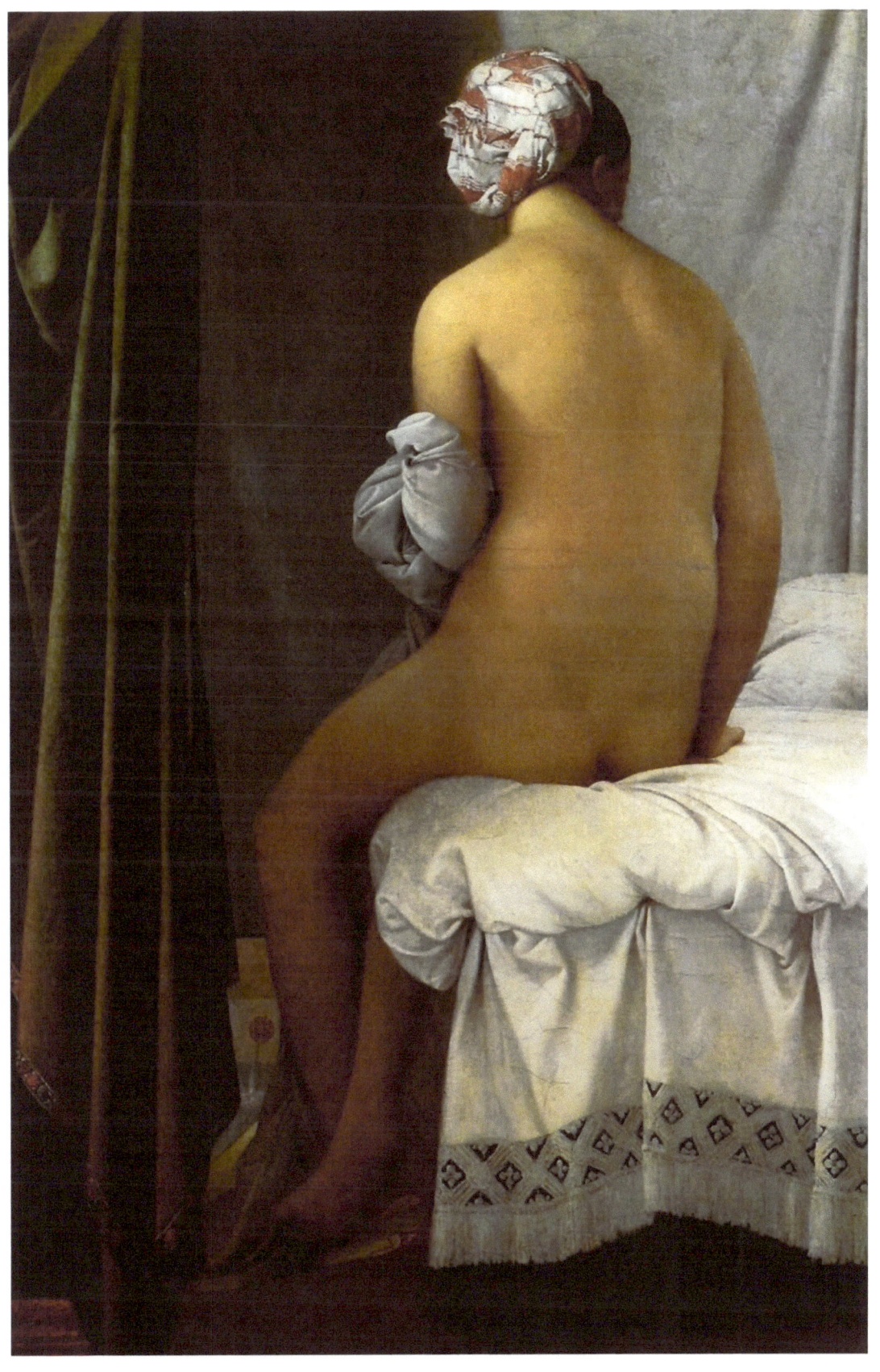

The Bather of Valpinçon

1808, oil on canvas

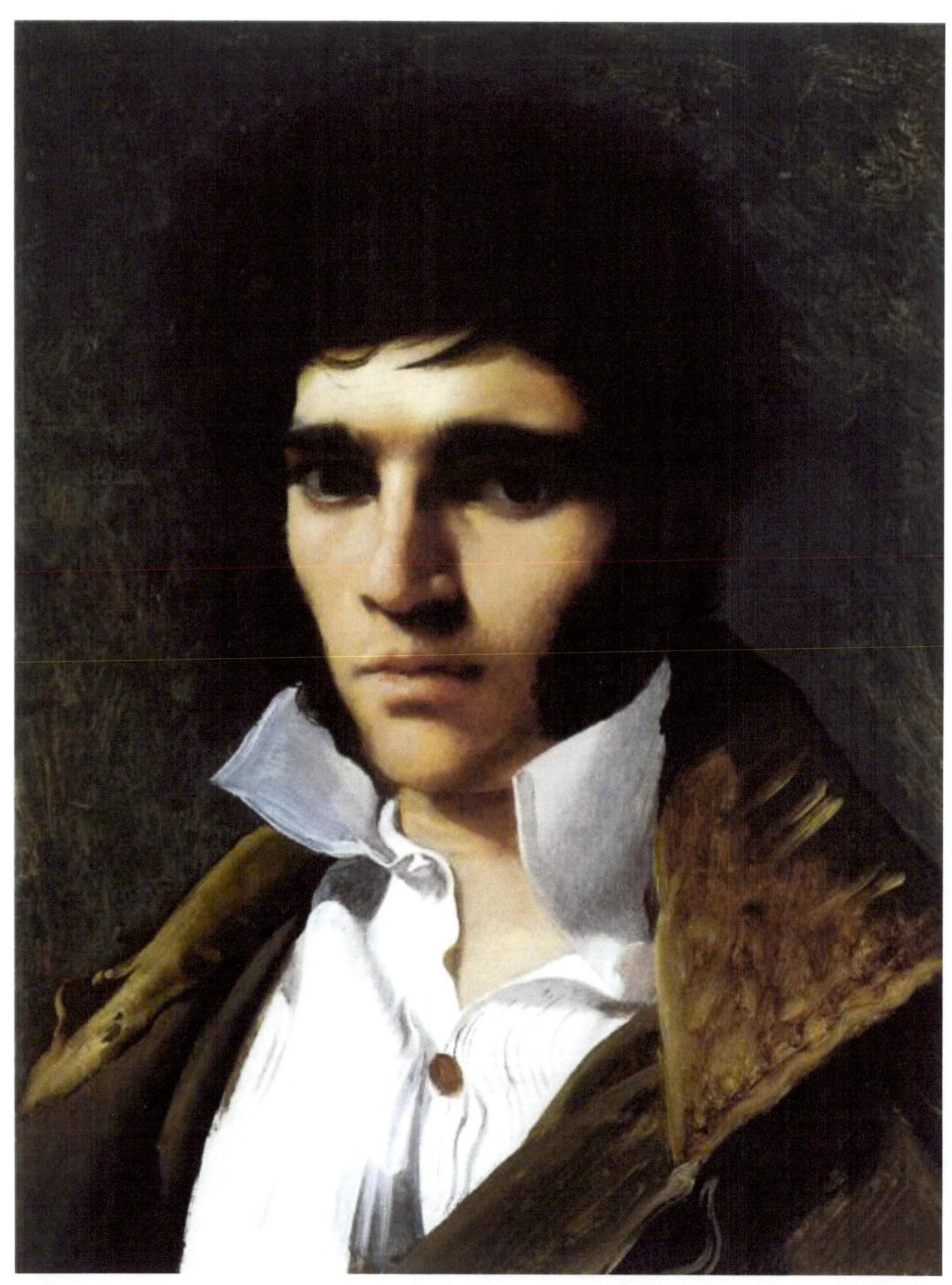

Paul Lemoyne

1810, oil on canvas

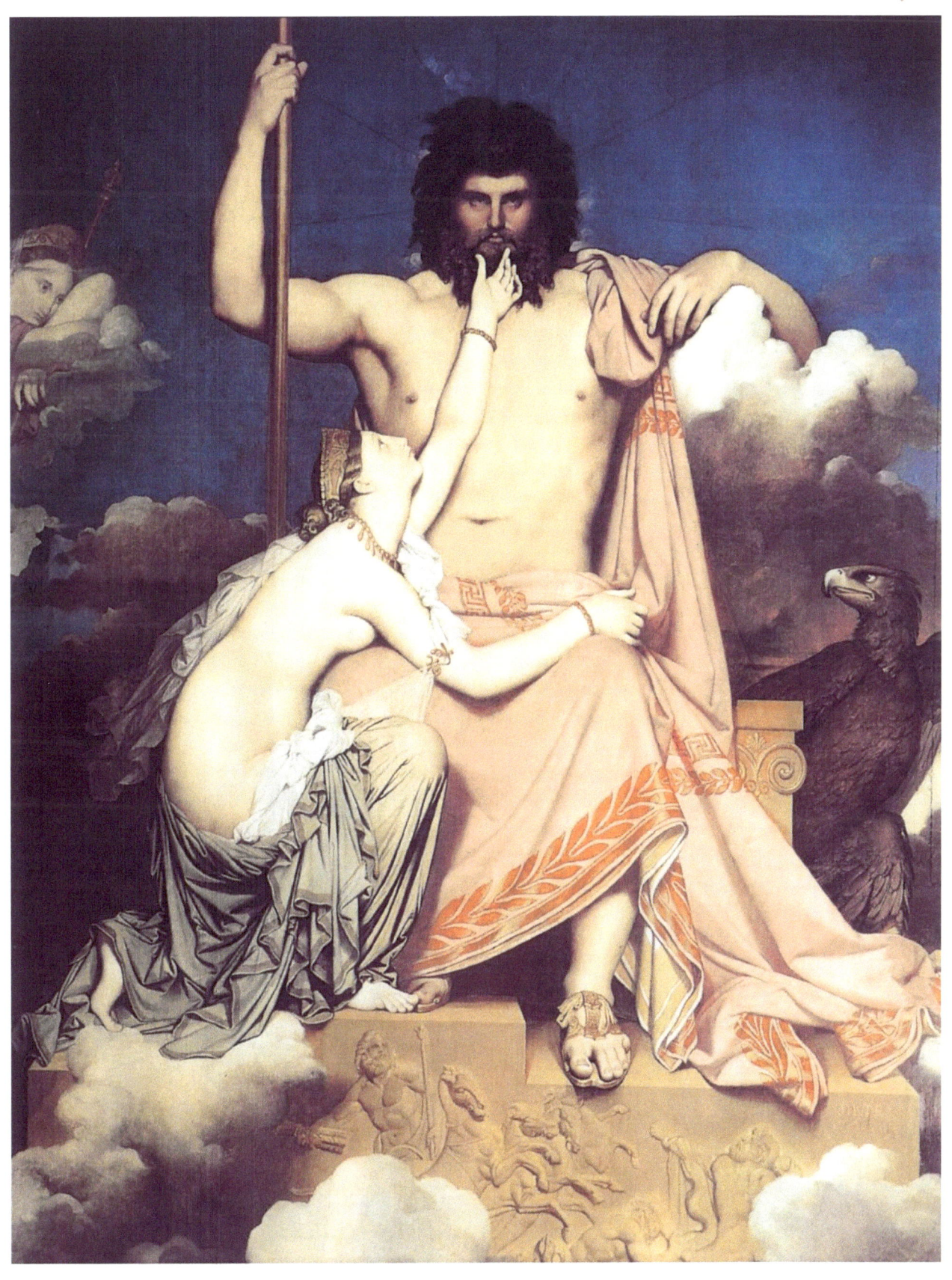

Jupiter and Thetis

1811, oil on canvas

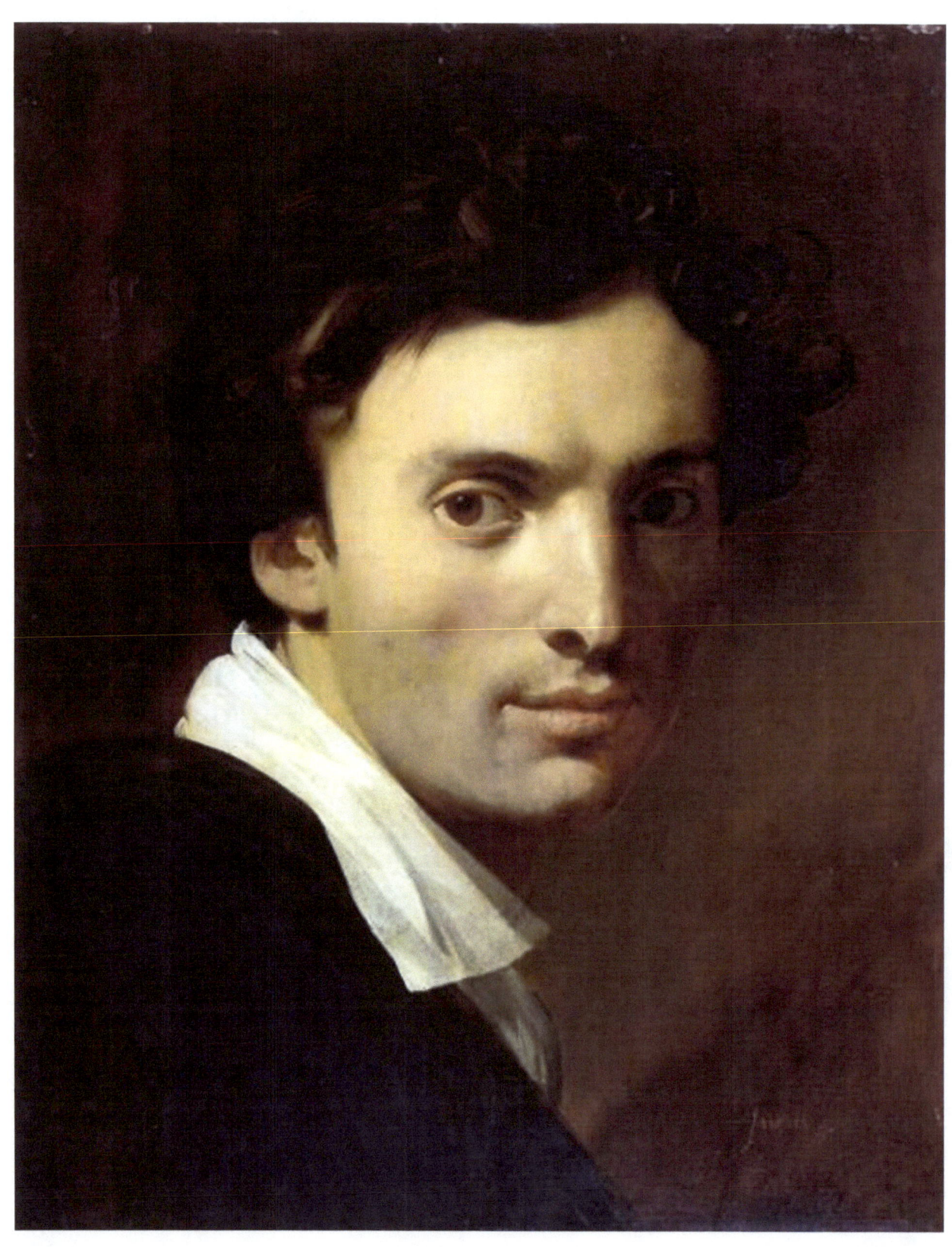

Jean Pierre Cortot

1815, oil on canvas

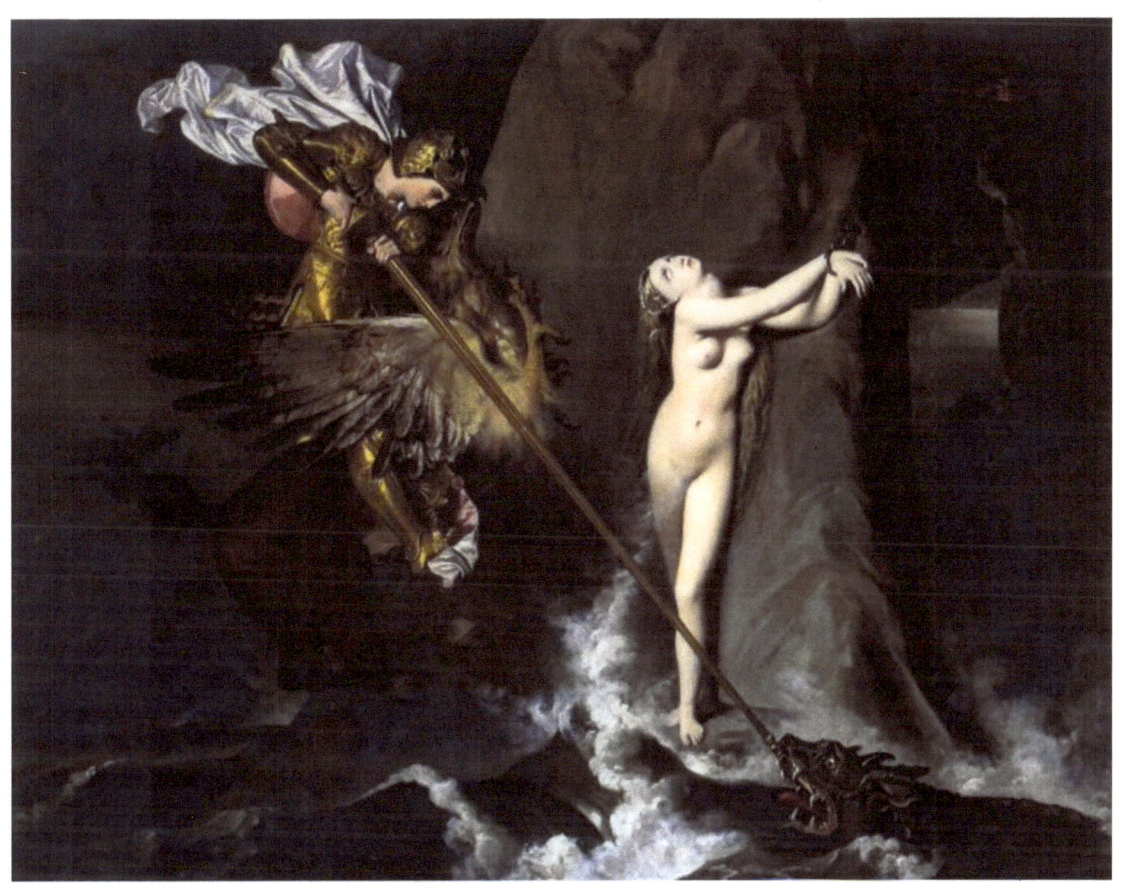

Roger Delivering Angelica

1819, oil on canvas

Angelica is the daughter of a king of Cathay in Orlando Furioso, by the Italian poet Ariosto (1474-1533), a romantic epic poem about the conflict between Christians and Saracens at the time of Charlemagne. Angelica was loved by several knights, Christian and pagan, among them the Christian hero Orlando (Roland). He was maddened (furioso) with grief and jealousy because she became the lover of, and eventually married, the Moor Modero. Roger (Ruggiero) freeing Angelica is a theme very like Perseus and Andromeda. Angelica chained to a rock by the seashore is about to be attacked by a sea-monster, the orc. Roger, one of the pagan champions, arrives riding on a hippogriff (a monster, the creation of the poets of the late middle ages). He dazzles the monster with his magic shield, and places a magic ring on Angelica's finger to protect her. He undoes her bonds and they ride off together.Ingres developed a highly sensitive aestheticism, particularly in depicting the beautiful naked body. He excelled his teachers in this, and it was here that he sought an ideal of form that goes to the limits of what can be done in painting. It is hard to find an equal anywhere in the history of art turned to us by The Grand Odalisque or the body of the young girl in Roger Freeing Angelica, modeled in soft lines.The position of the young Angelica, with her head tilted back, is highly exaggerated by modern standards, but the exposed and defenseless neck and the eyes cast up to suggest that she has fainted are intended to signalise pure feminine submission. In order to portray this unconditional surrender to her rescuer, Ingres has almost made her look as if she has goitre. But this calculated submission to the aesthetic of the nude makes it no less erotic precisely because the very evidence of a weak spot in her beauty makes her seem less remote from the viewer.

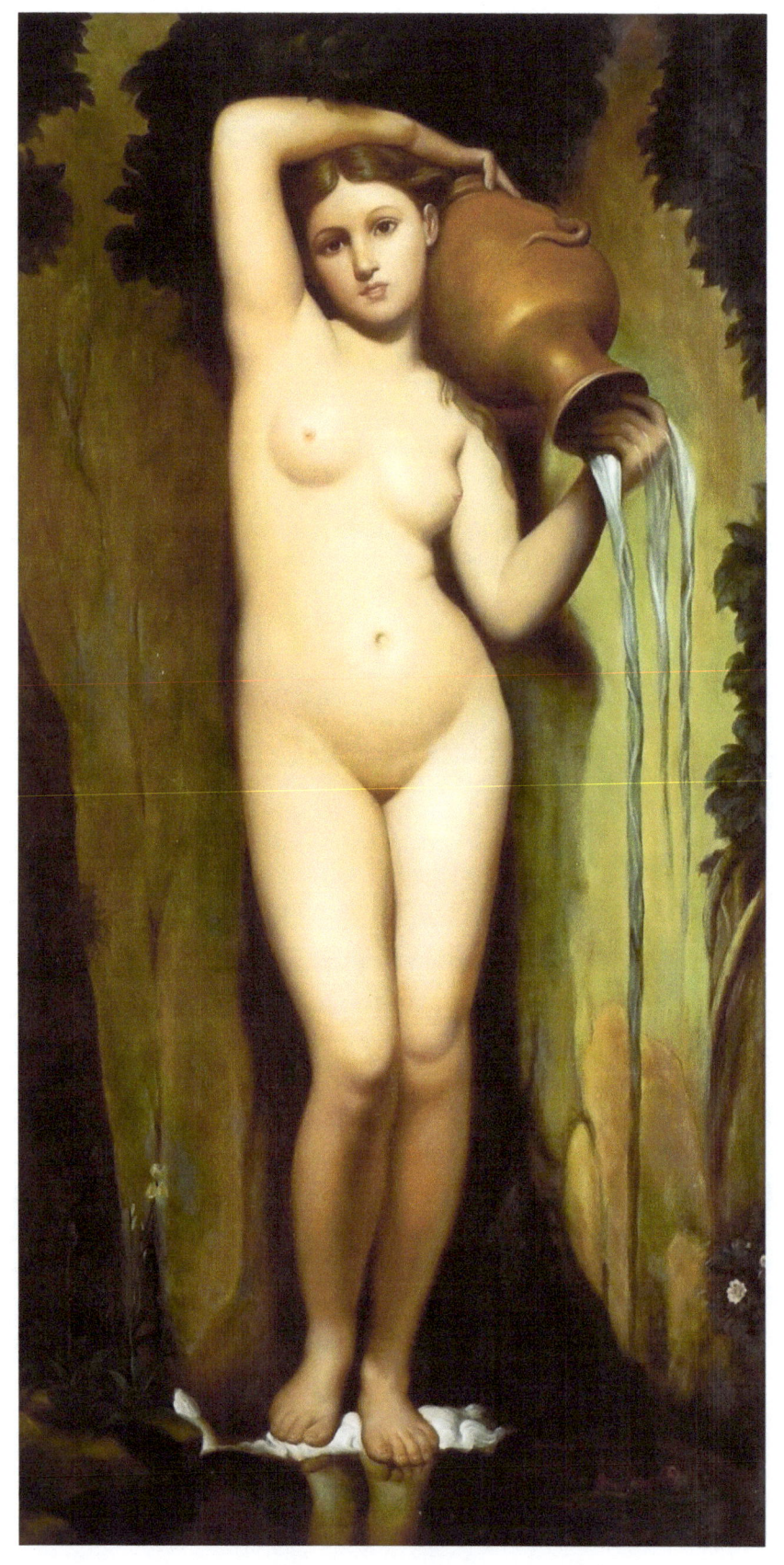

The Source

1820, Oil on canvas, 83 x 163 cm

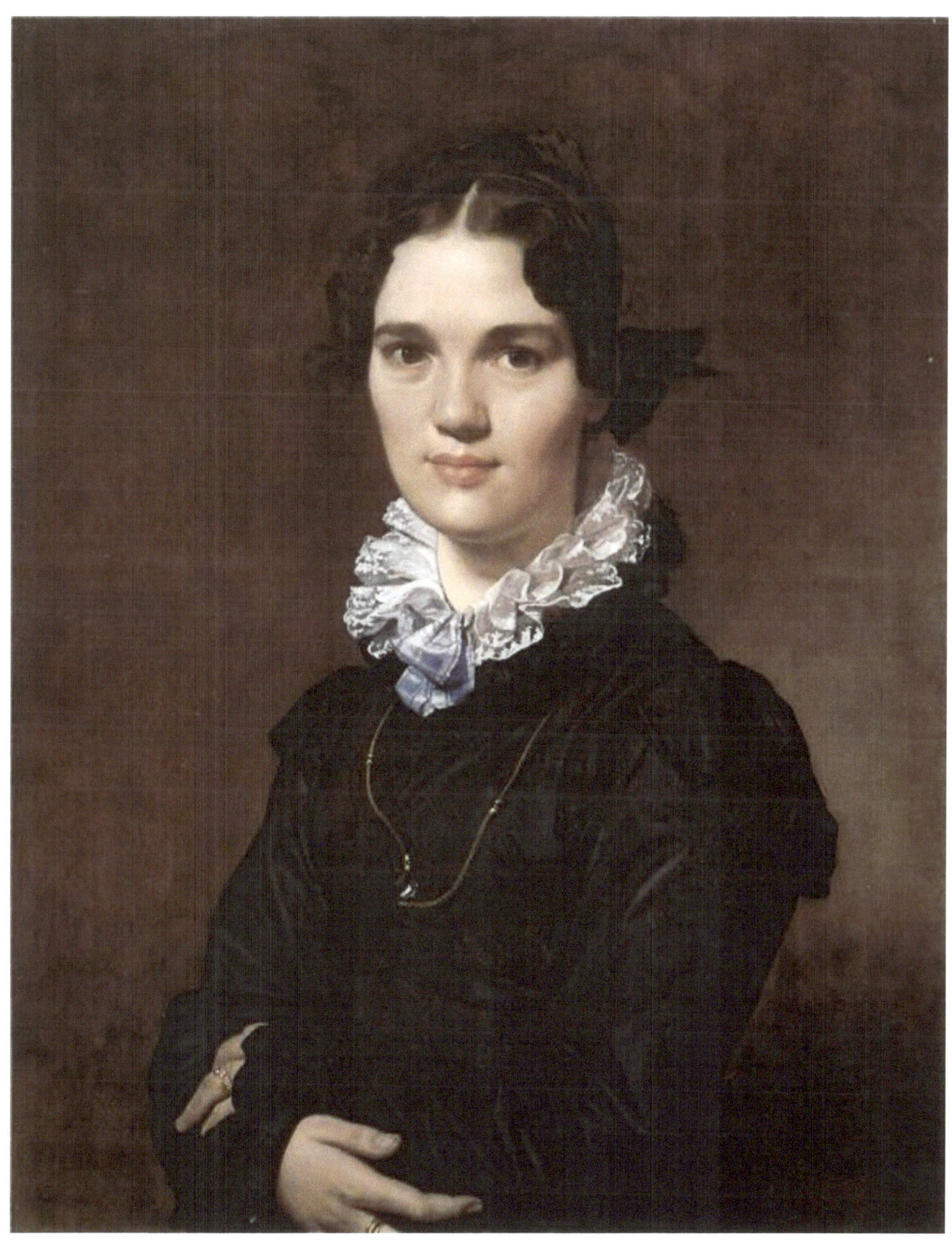

Mademoiselle Jeanne Gonin

1821, oil on canvas

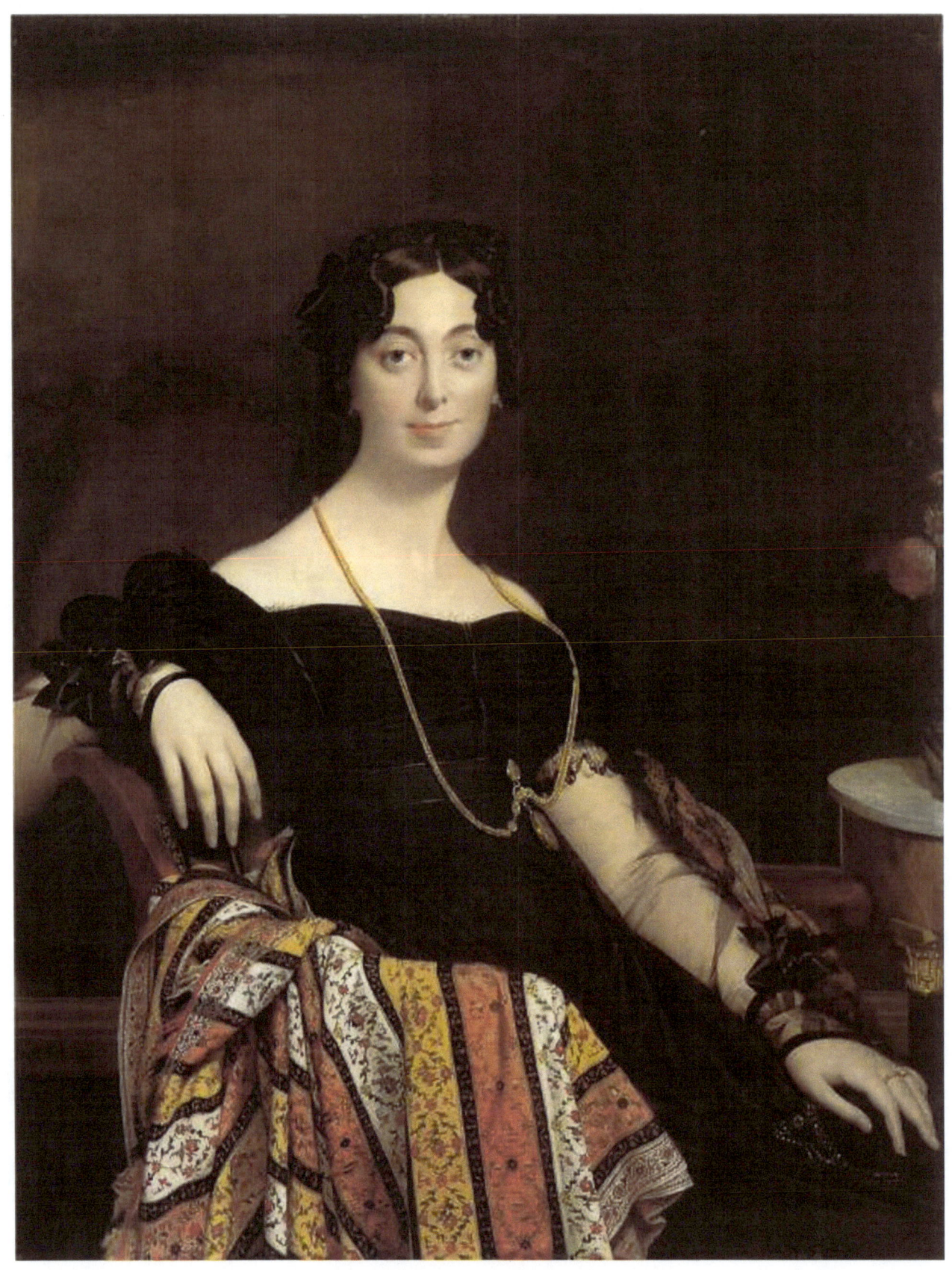

Portrait of Madame Leblanc

1823, oil on canvas

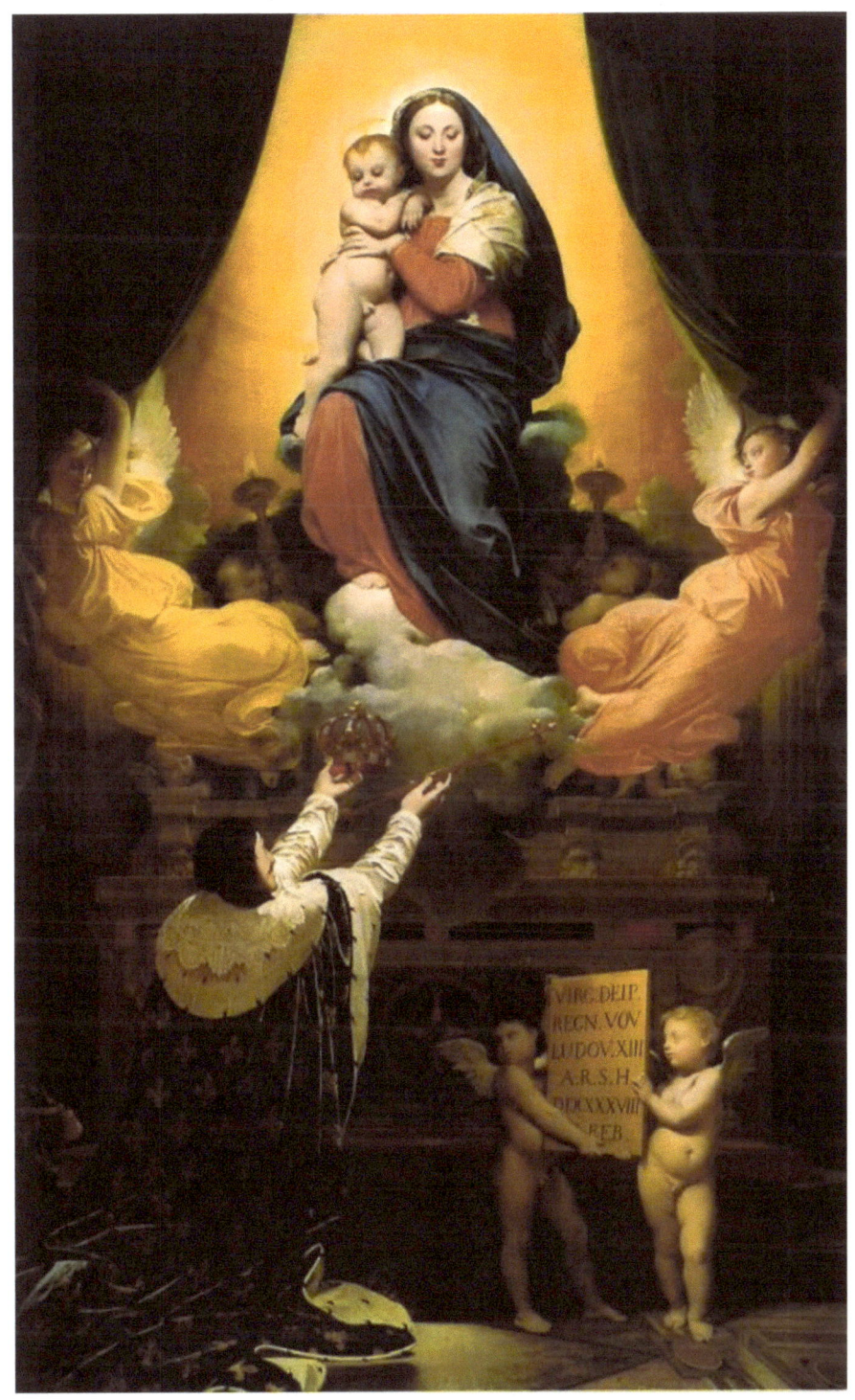

The Vow of Louis XIII

1824, oil on canvas

Ingres continued to paint in the Neoclassical style throughout his career, although the style came under attack from younger contemporaries like Gŭricault or Delacroix. The Vow of Louis XIII is a kind of neoclassical votive painting. In it Ingres adapted whole passages of Raphael's Madonna di Foligno, but he also borrowed forms that were developed by the Carraccis.

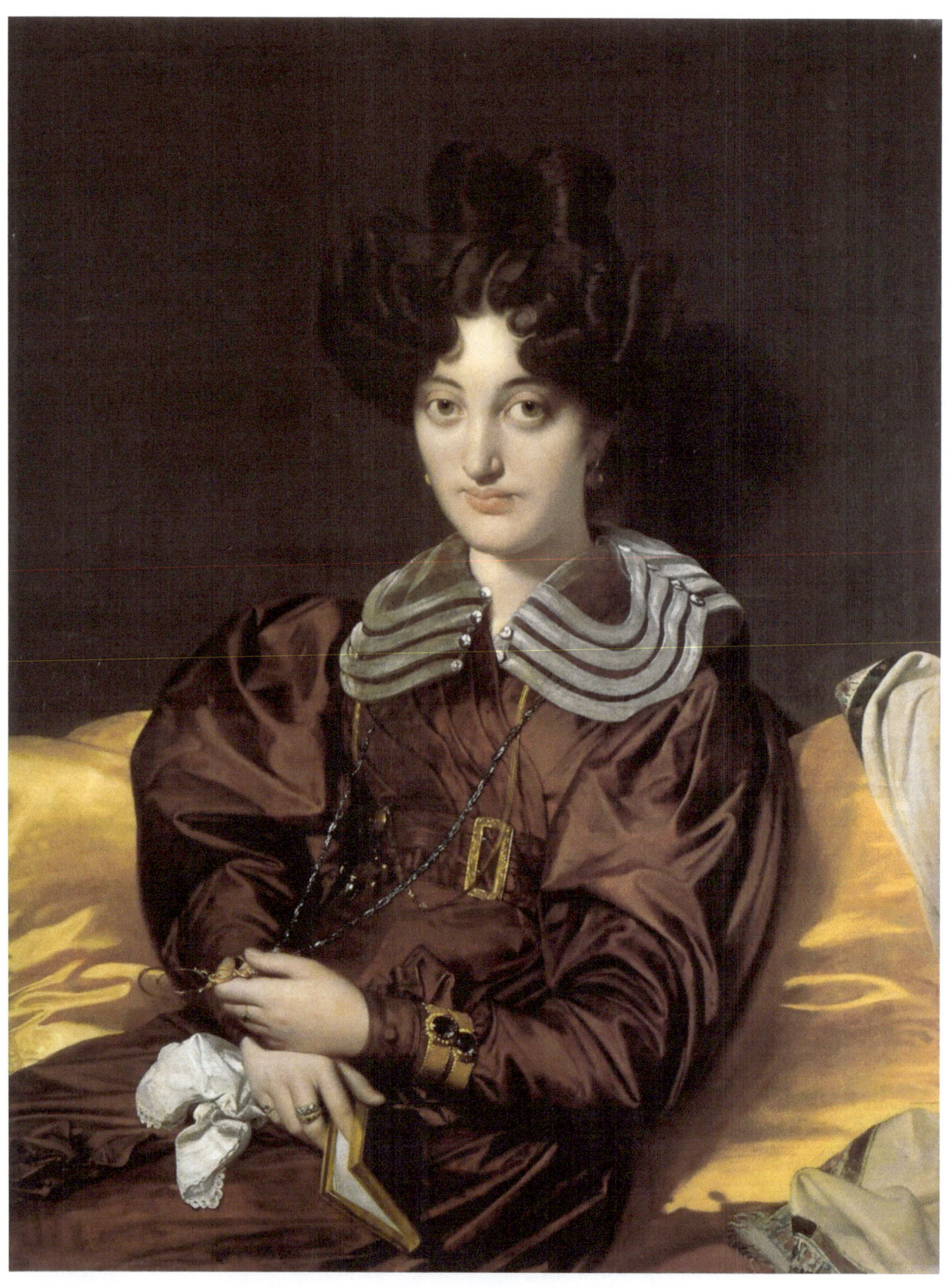

Portrait of Madame Marcotte de Sainte-Marie

1826, oil on canvas

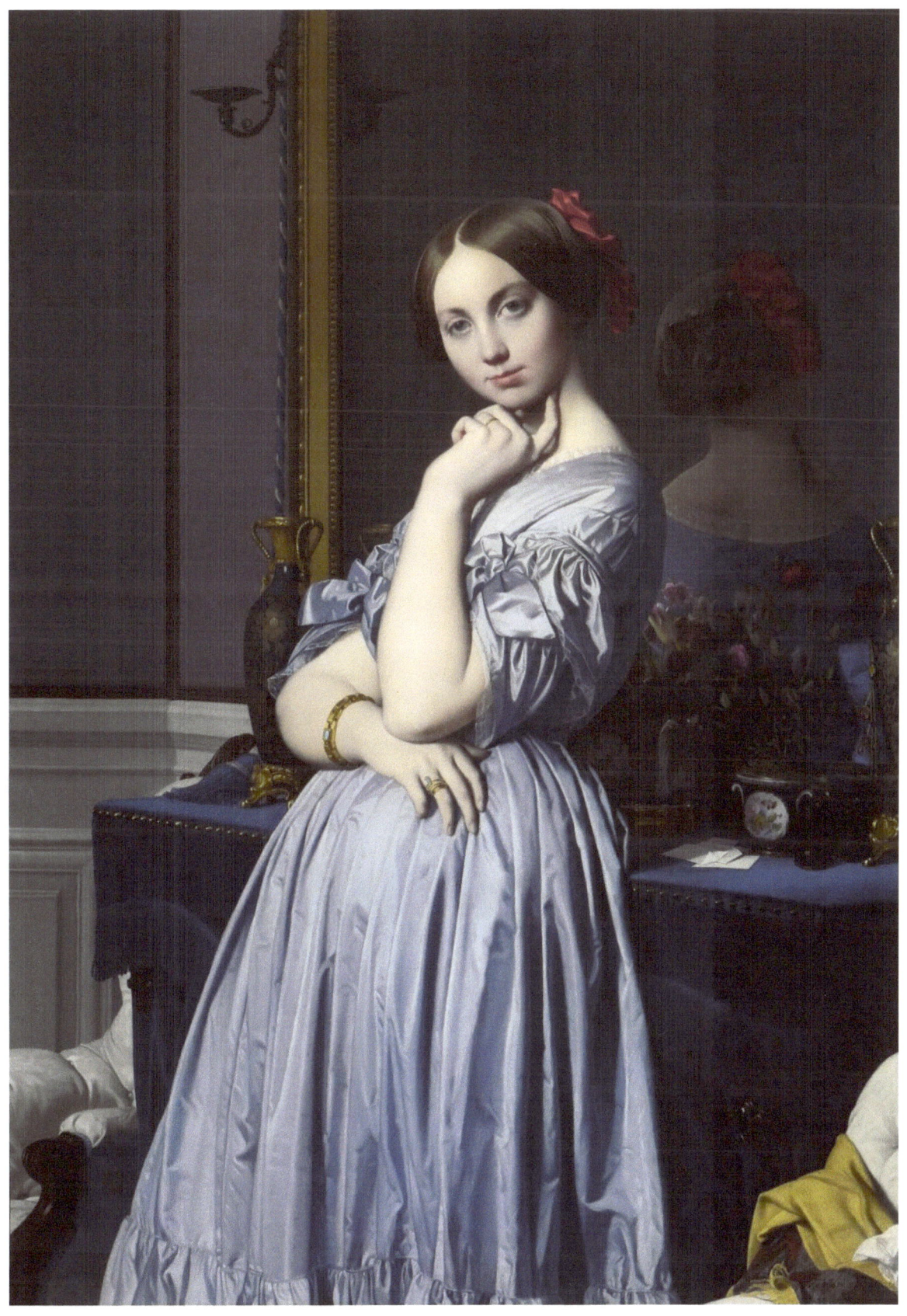

Portrait of Countess D'Haussonville

1845, oil on canvas

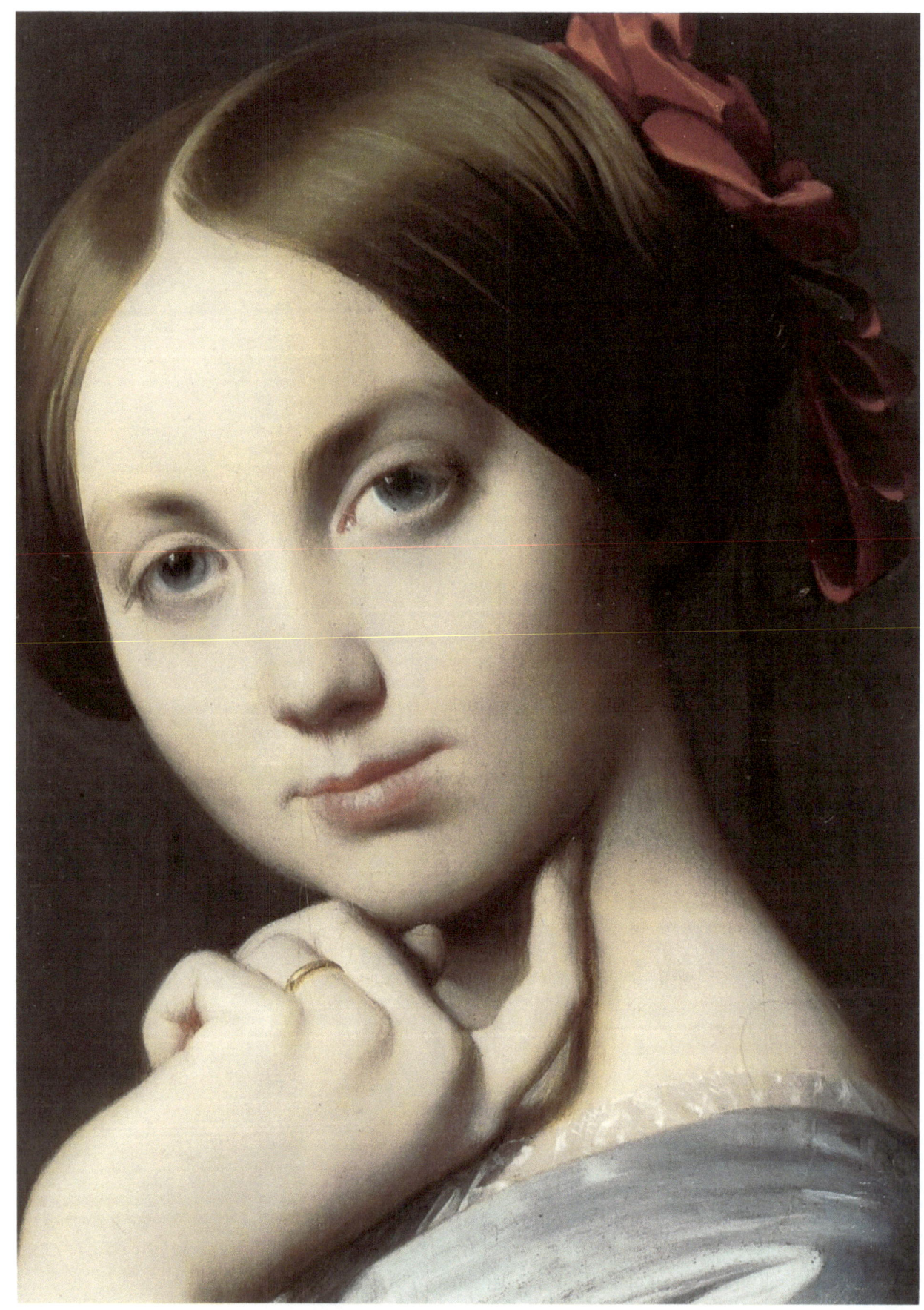

Detail

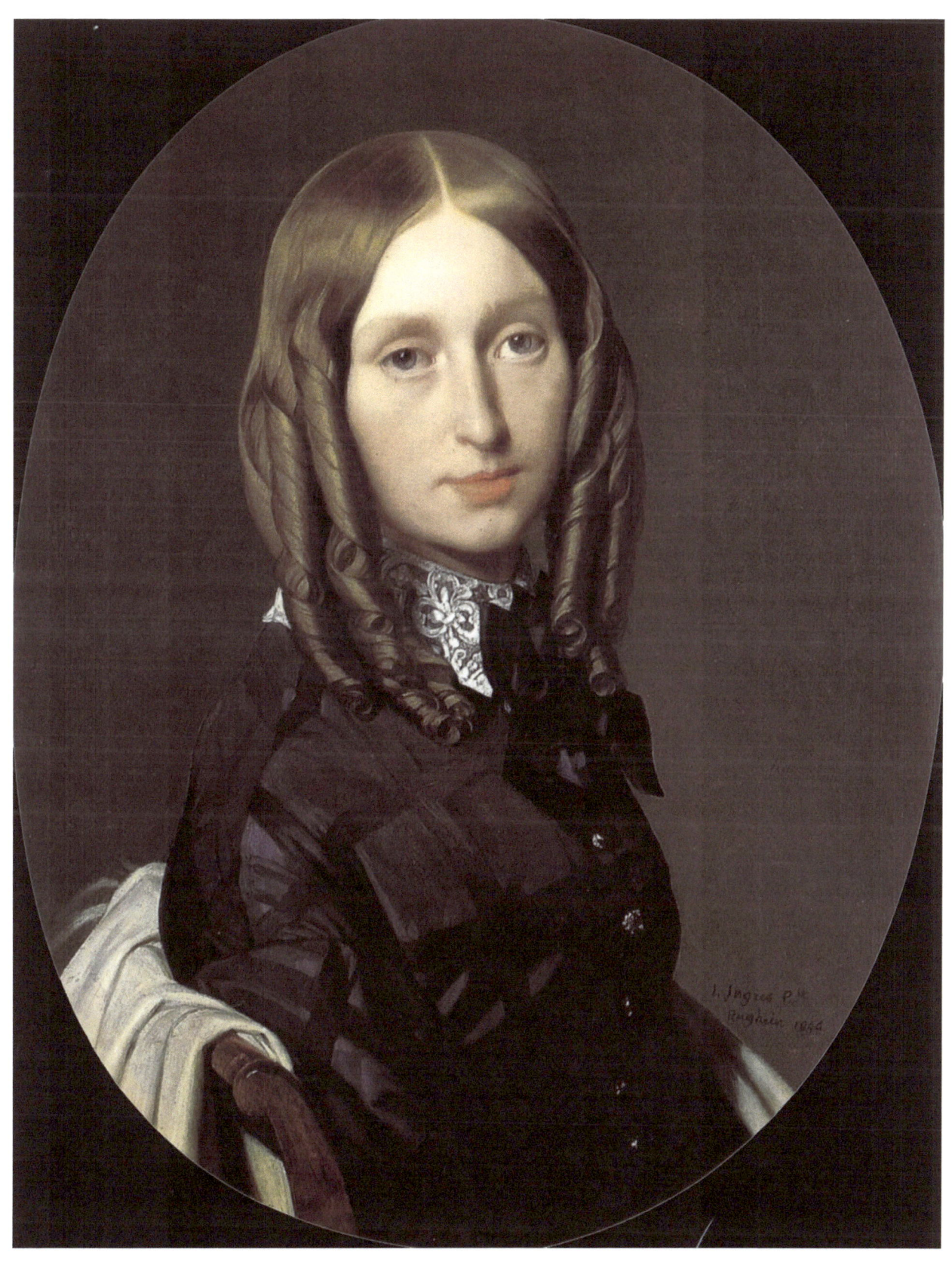

Portrait of Madame Frederic Reiset

1846-1847, oil on canvas

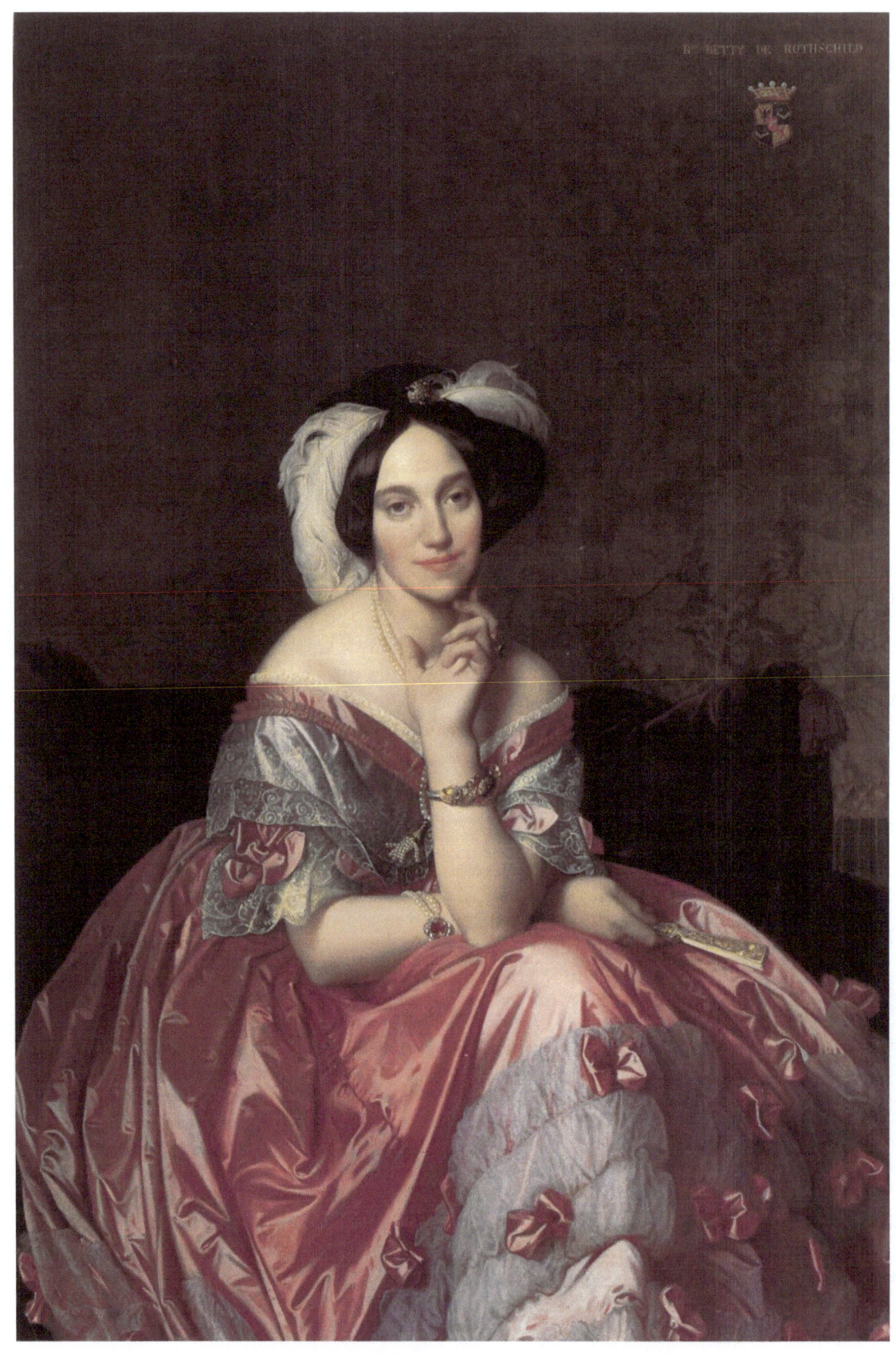

Baronesss Betty de Rothschild

1848, oil on canvas

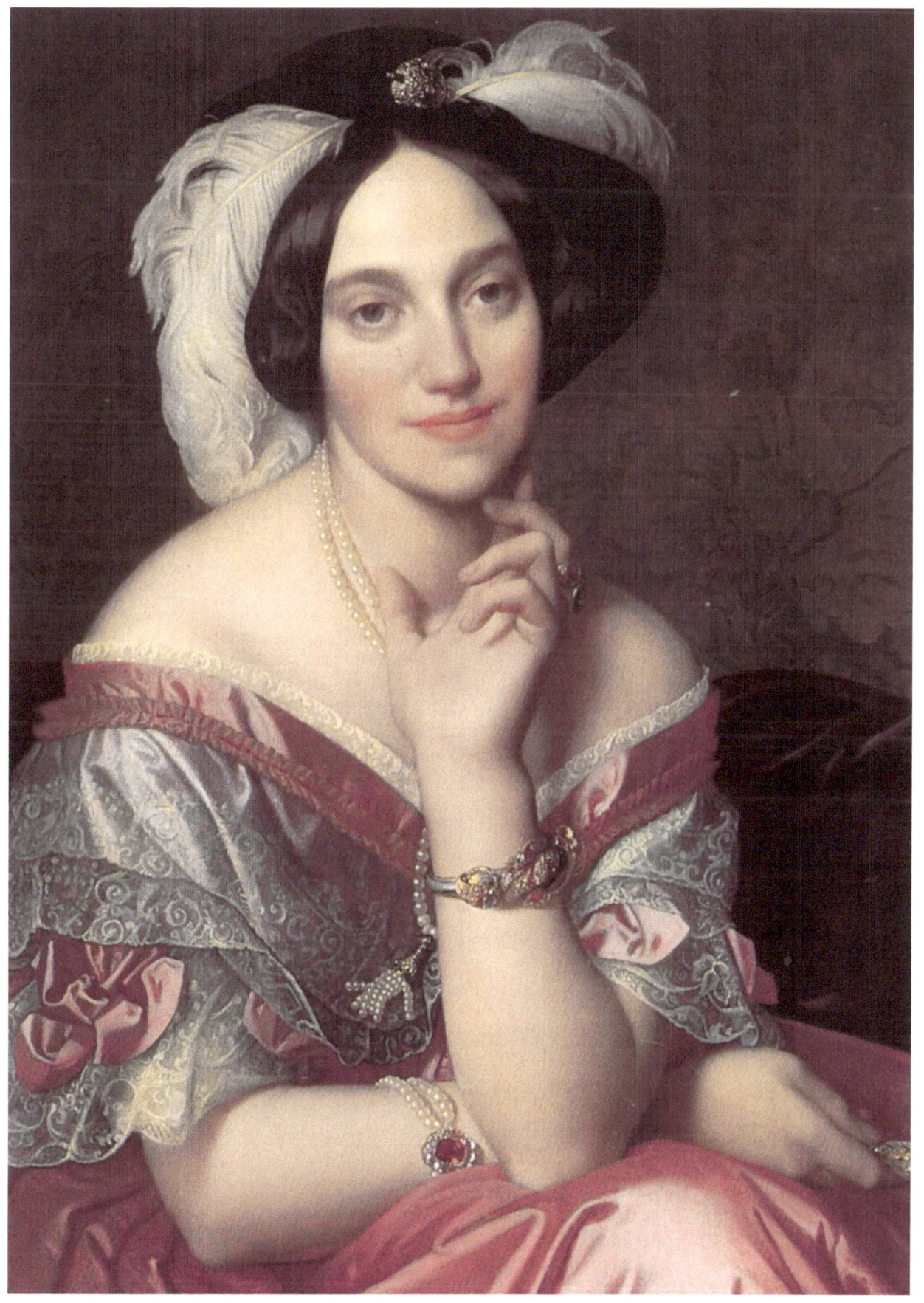

Detail

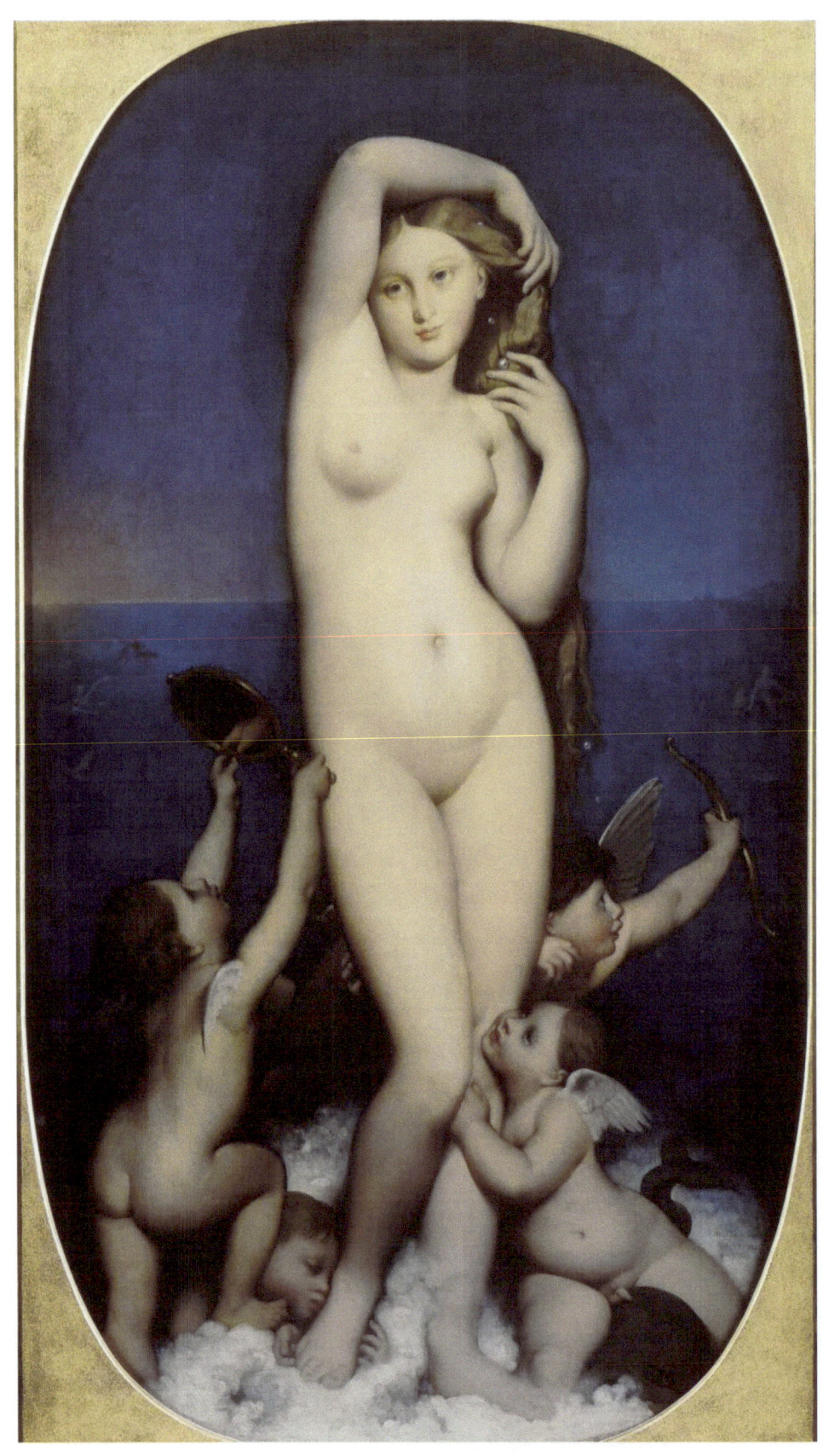

Venus Anadyomene

1848, oil on canvas

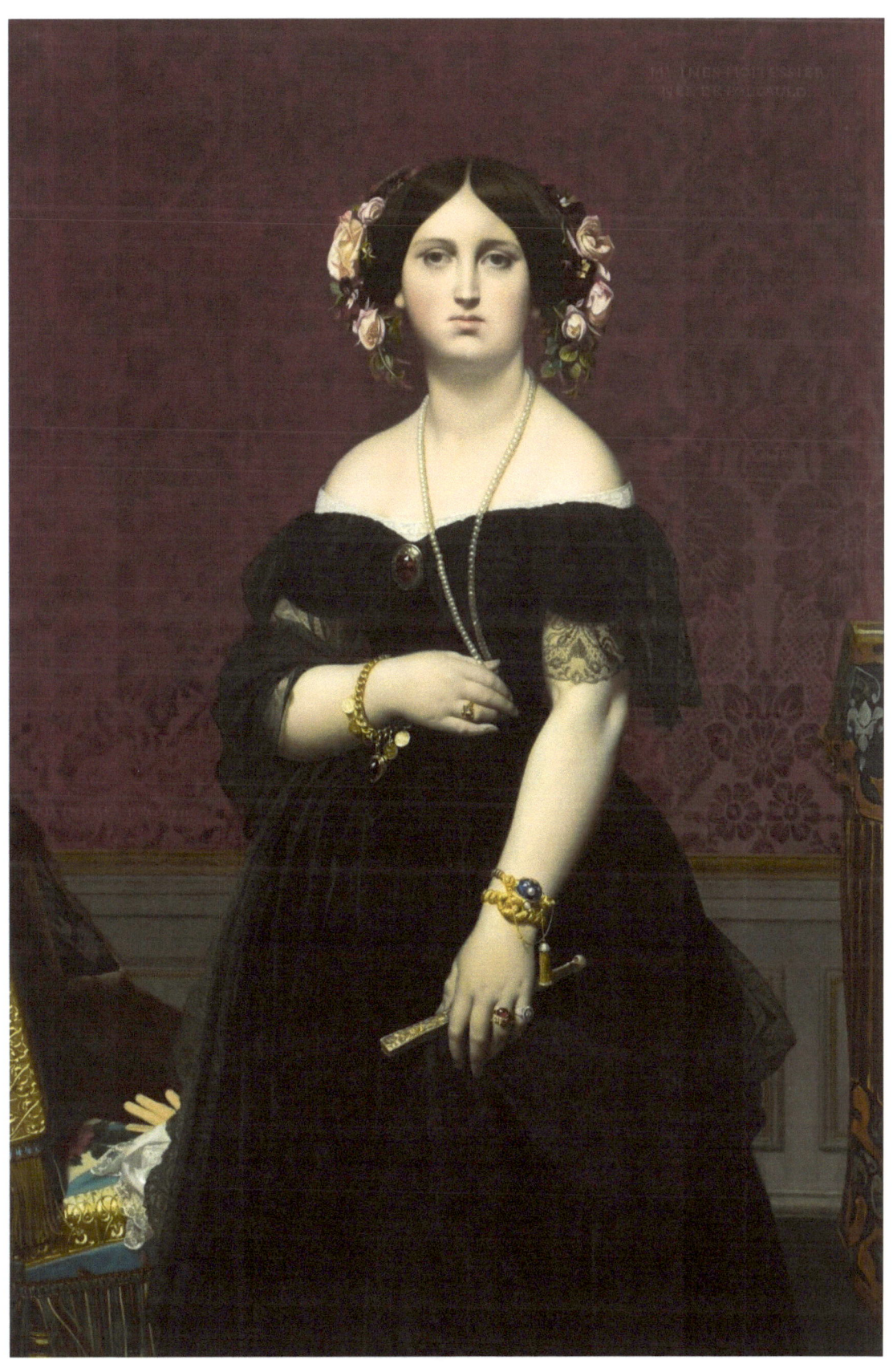

Portrait of Madame Moitessier Standing

1851, oil on canvas

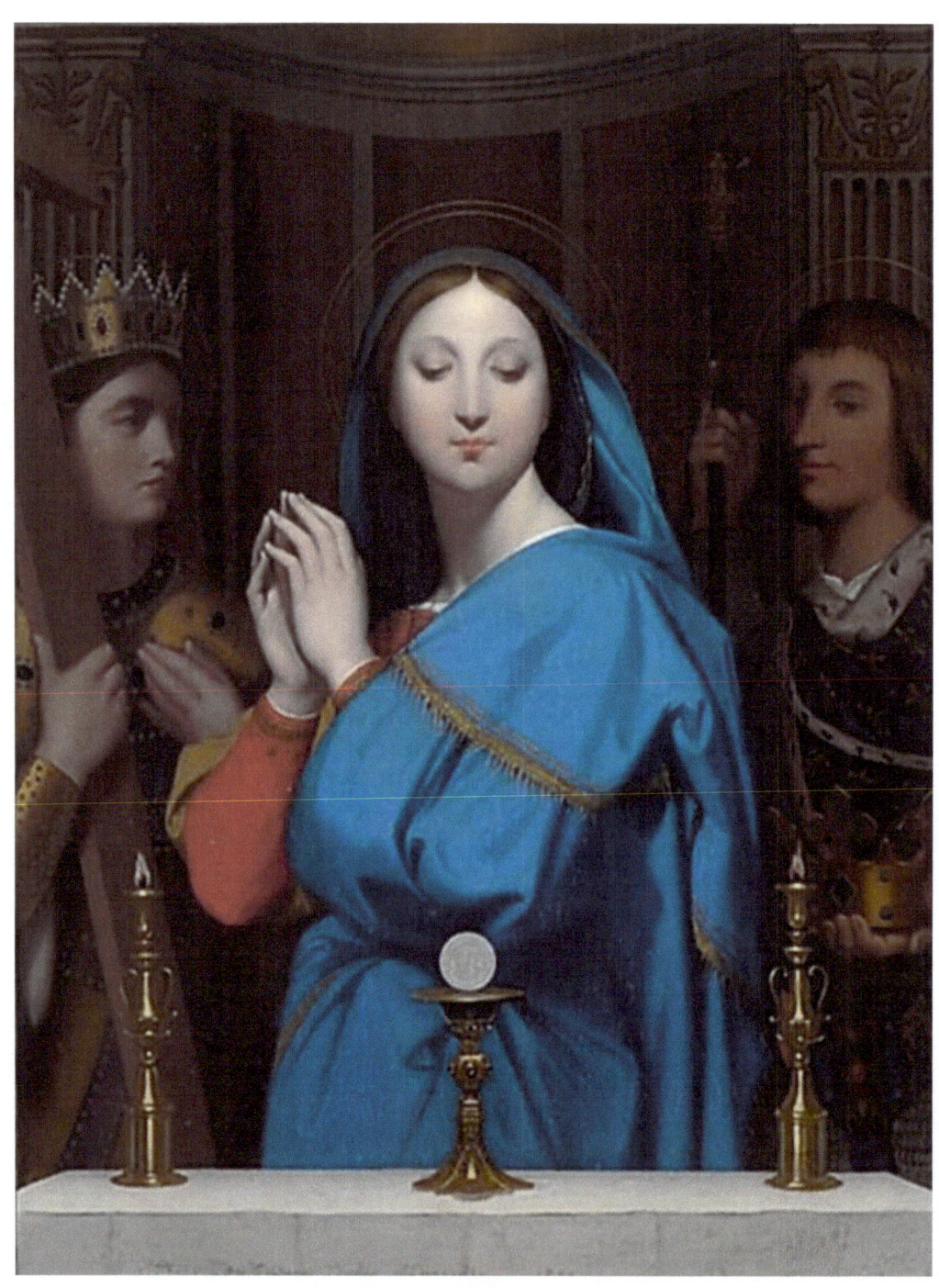

The Virgin Adoring the Host

1852, oil on canvas

This small, jewel-like devotional painting was made as a gift for Ingres's friend Louise Marcotte, who introduced the artist to Delphine Ramel, whom he married in 1852. The Raphaelesque composition is based on one Ingres first painted in 1841 for the future czar Alexander II, which includes the two patron saints of Russia, Alexander Nevsky and Nicholas (Pushkin Museum of Fine Arts, Moscow). For this version, Ingres replaced the Russian saints with two French ones. He would go on to paint four more variants, as well as, in 1855, a watercolor for Madame Ingres herself.

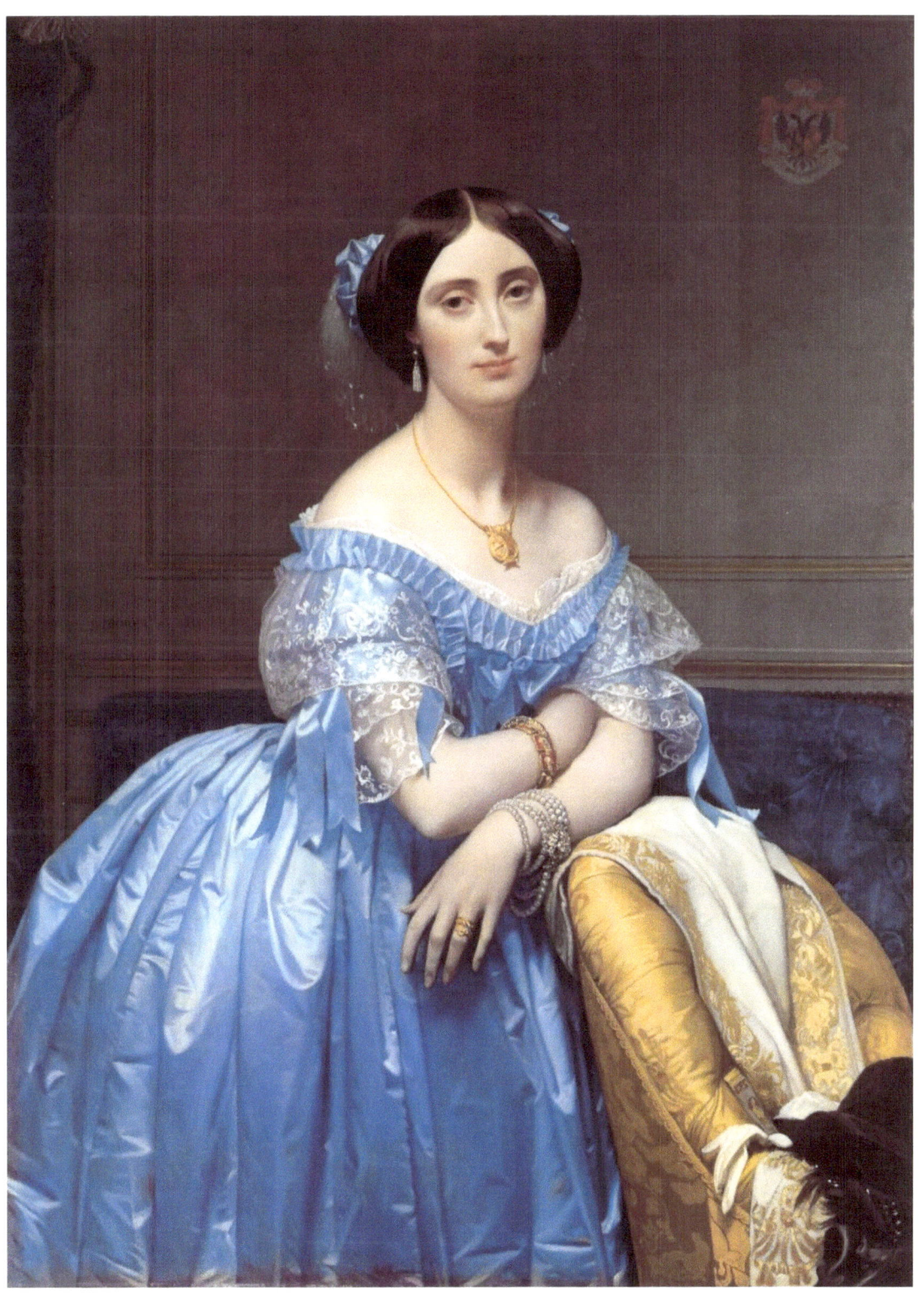

Portrait of the Princesse de Broglie

1853, oil on canvas

The princesse de Broglie (1825-1860) was a great beauty and a highly respected woman, the embodiment of the best of the Second Empire aristocracy. Ingres began her portrait in 1851; after accepting the commission he wrote to a friend that it would be his last except for that of his wife.

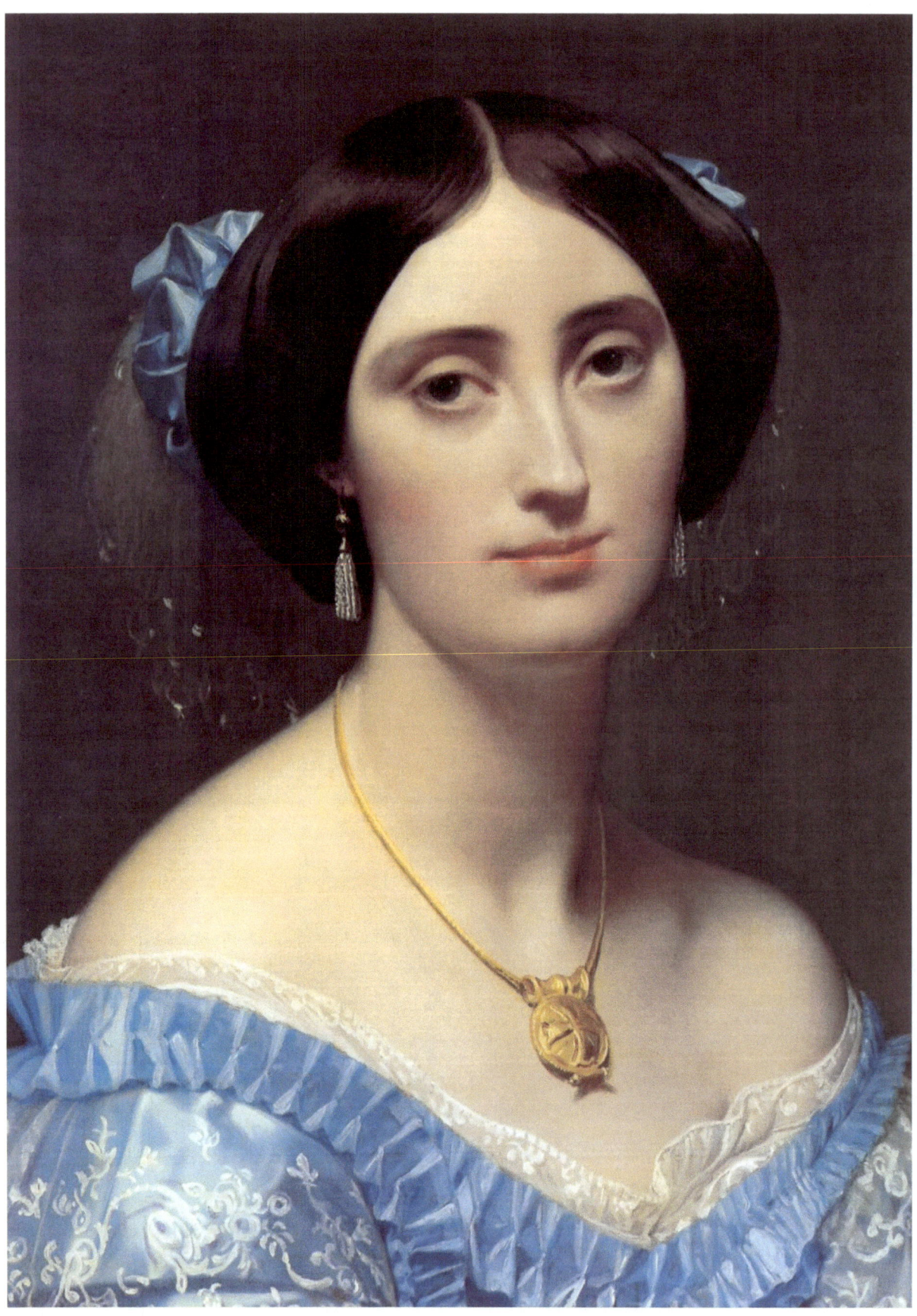

Detail

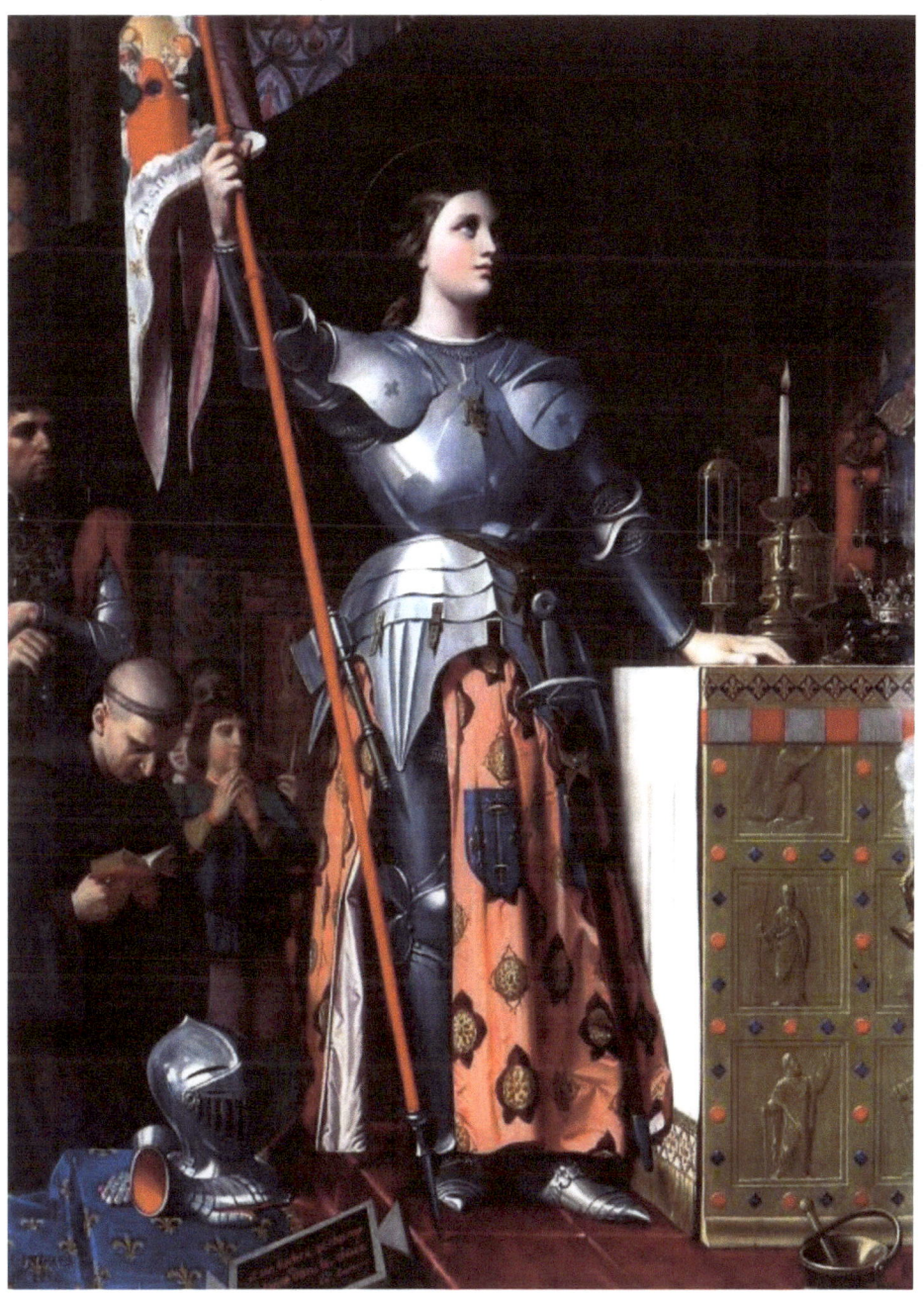

Joan of Arc on Corronation of Charles VII in the Cathedral of Reims

1854, oil on canvas

Charles VII (1403-1461) was a monarch of the House of Valois who ruled as King of France from 1422 to his death. In 1422, Charles VII inherited the throne of France under desperate circumstances. Forces of the Kingdom of England and the Duchy of Burgundy occupied Guyenne and northern France, including Paris, the most populous city, and Reims, the city in which the French kings were traditionally crowned. His political and military position improved dramatically with the emergence of Joan of Arc as a spiritual leader in France. Joan and other charismatic military leaders led French troops to several important victories that paved the way for the coronation of Charles VII in 1429 at Reims Cathedral.

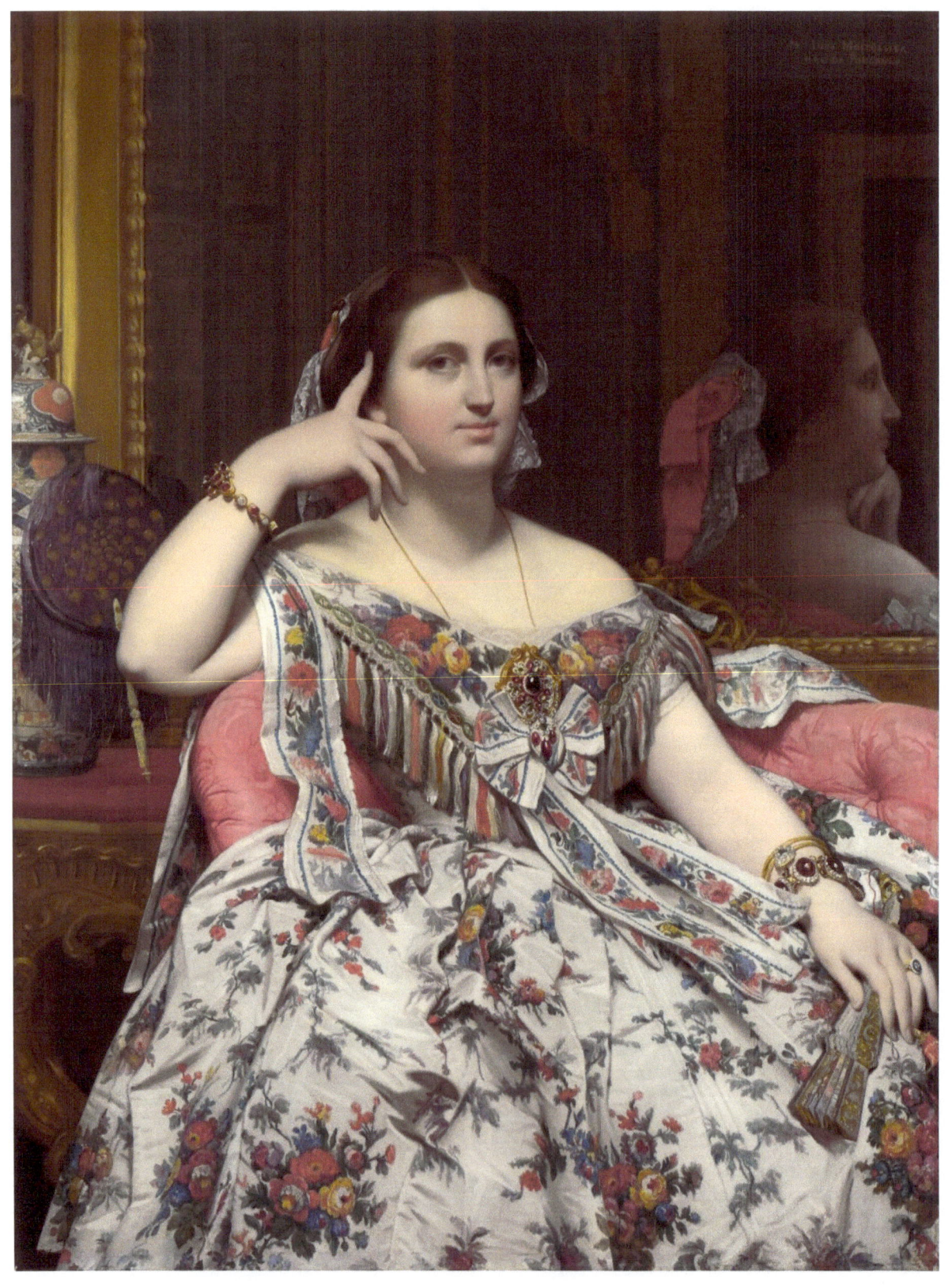

Madame Moitessier

1856, Oil on canvas, 120 x 92 cm

It is often said that while Delacroix was the great proponent of French Romanticism, his older contemporary Ingres was the champion of the classical tradition: obsessed with Raphael and antiquity, upholder of 'drawing' versus 'colour'. Real life being less tidy, however, we find that Delacroix was a more calculating artist than the hyper-emotional Ingres, who did not hesitate to break academic rules for expressive ends. Both painted subjects from literature and history, and his response to the female nude is as charged with erotic longing and scarcely sublimated violence as Delacroix's. Nor did Ingres invariably emulate Raphael and Poussin. Throughout his long career he tried to match style to subject, looking in turn to Greek vase painting, to the Early Renaissance, even to the Dutch seventeenth-century painters of everyday life.

It is, however, true that drawing was of primary importance to him. Forced to support himself and his wife in Rome in 1814 by drawing the English tourists who flocked back to the city liberated from French rule, he developed a wonderfully spare, yet lively and descriptive line. Although he despised portraiture as a lower form of art, like his teacher David Ingres came to excel in it. Few of his painted portraits are more sumptuous than Madame Moitessier, begun in 1847 but completed only in 1856 when the artist, as he tells us in his signature, was 76.

He had originally refused to paint this wealthy banker's wife, but when he met her he was so captivated by her beauty that he agreed, asking her to bring her small daughter, 'la charmante Catherine', whose head is visible under her mother's arm in a preparatory drawing in the Ingres Museum in Montauban. The doubtless bored and wriggling child was soon banished as Ingres wrestled with the picture, requiring long hours of immobility from his model. The sitter's dress was changed more than once. Ingres is recorded as still working on the portrait in 1847. The death of his wife in 1849 left him in despair and unable to paint for many months. In 1851 he began sittings anew and completed a standing likeness of Inns Moitessier in black (now in Washington). He returned to the seated version in 1852.

When he had finished four years later the sitter was 35. Ageless like a goddess with her Grecian profile impossibly reflected in a mirror parallel to the back of her head but dressed with Second Empire opulence in flowered chintz, Madame Moitessier exemplifies the ambiguities of Ingres's art. The firm contour of her shoulders, arms and face defines flesh perfectly rounded - though barely modelled - and as poreless, smooth and luminous as polished alabaster, yet paradoxically soft to the touch. In contrast to the resiliently buxom horsehair settee, it arouses fantasies and fears of bruising. The pose, with head resting against the right forefinger, derives from an ancient wall painting and signifies as Ingres must have known matronly modesty. But 'classicising' devices are offset by the minutely realistic transcription of the surfaces of fabrics, the fashionable parure of jewels, ormolu frames, Oriental porcelain. The mixture of the general with the particular, timeless grandeur with bourgeois ostentation, languor with pictorial rigour, is unique to Ingres and far from bloodlessly Neo-classical.

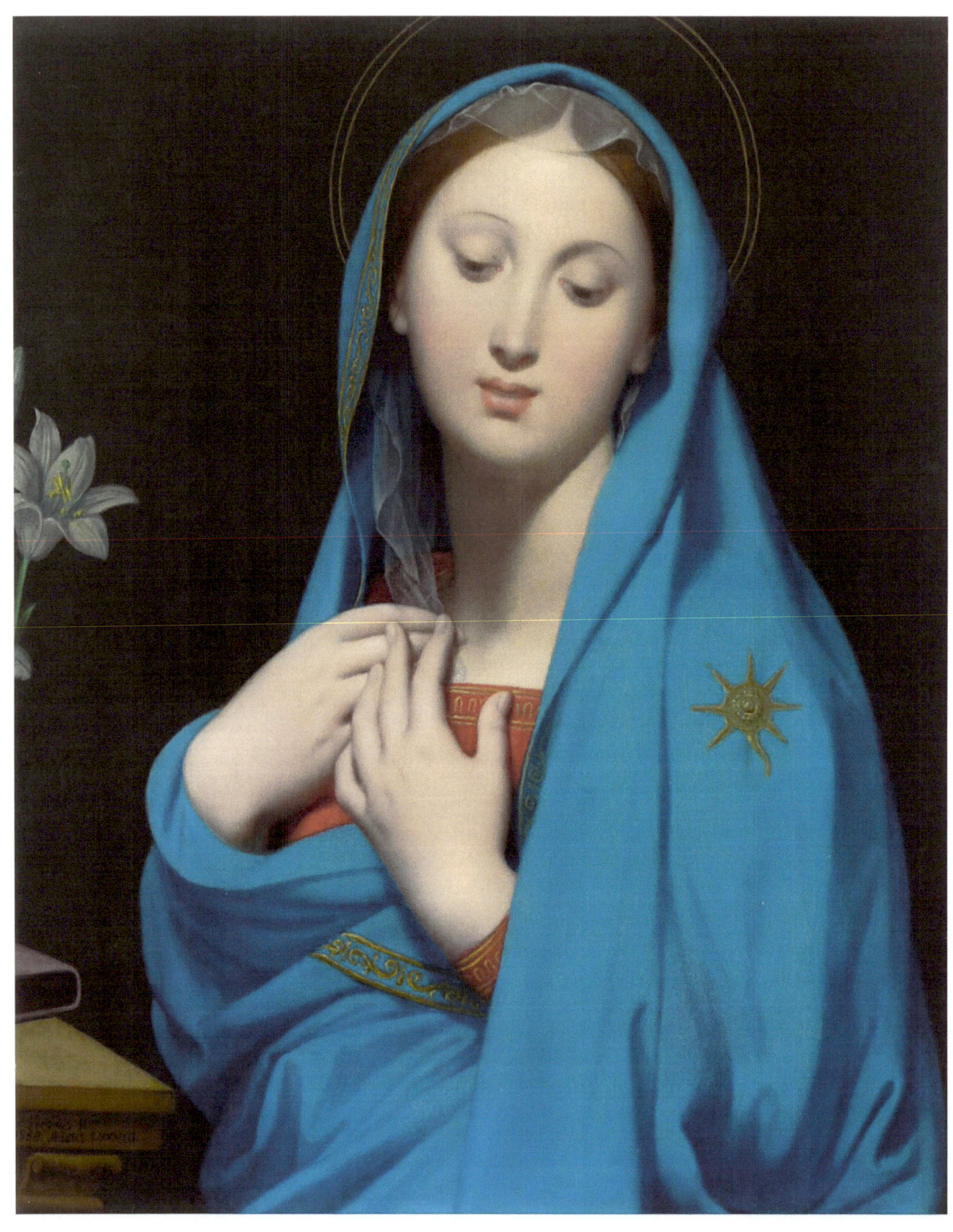

Virgin of the Adoption

1858, oil on canvas

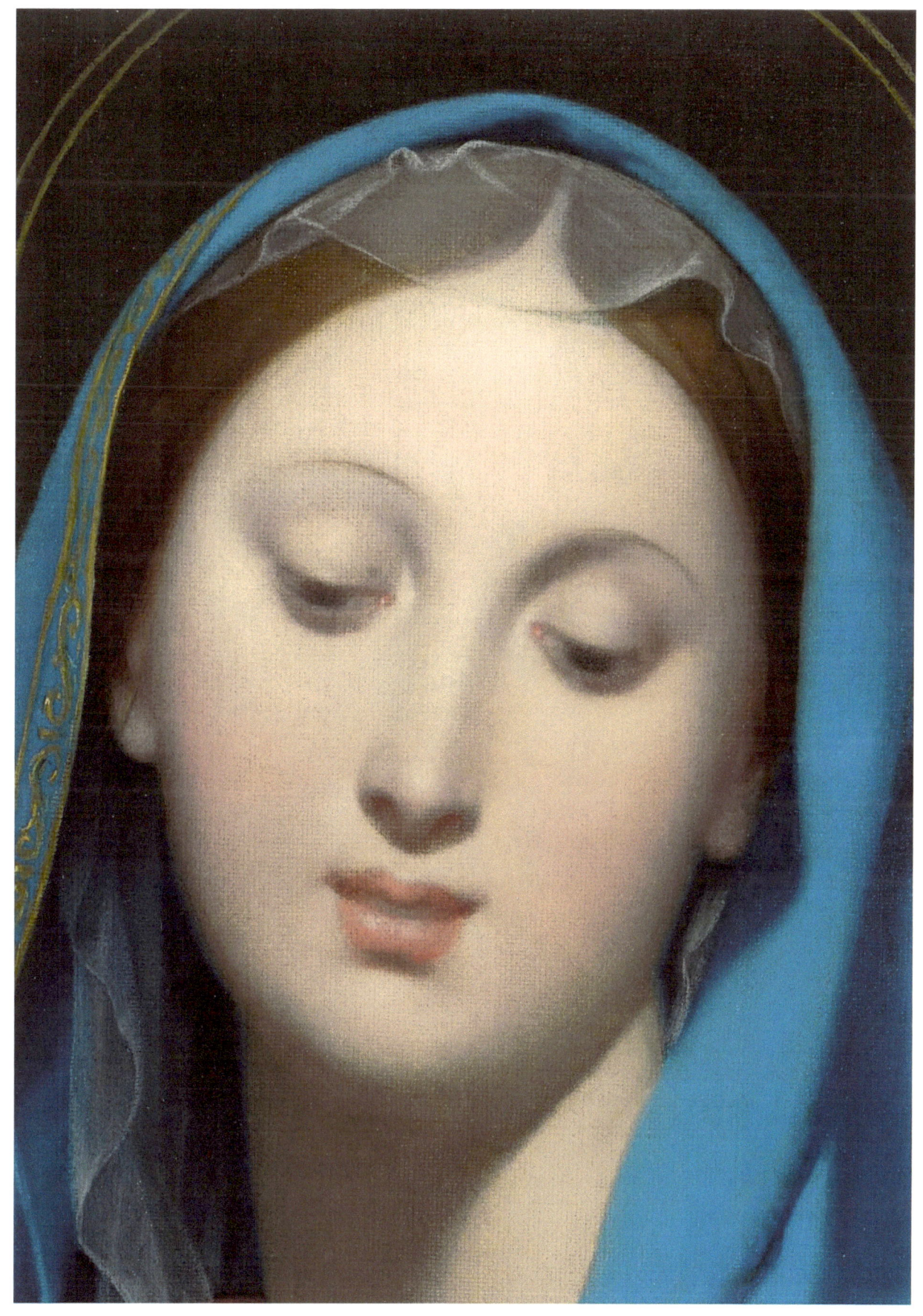

Detail

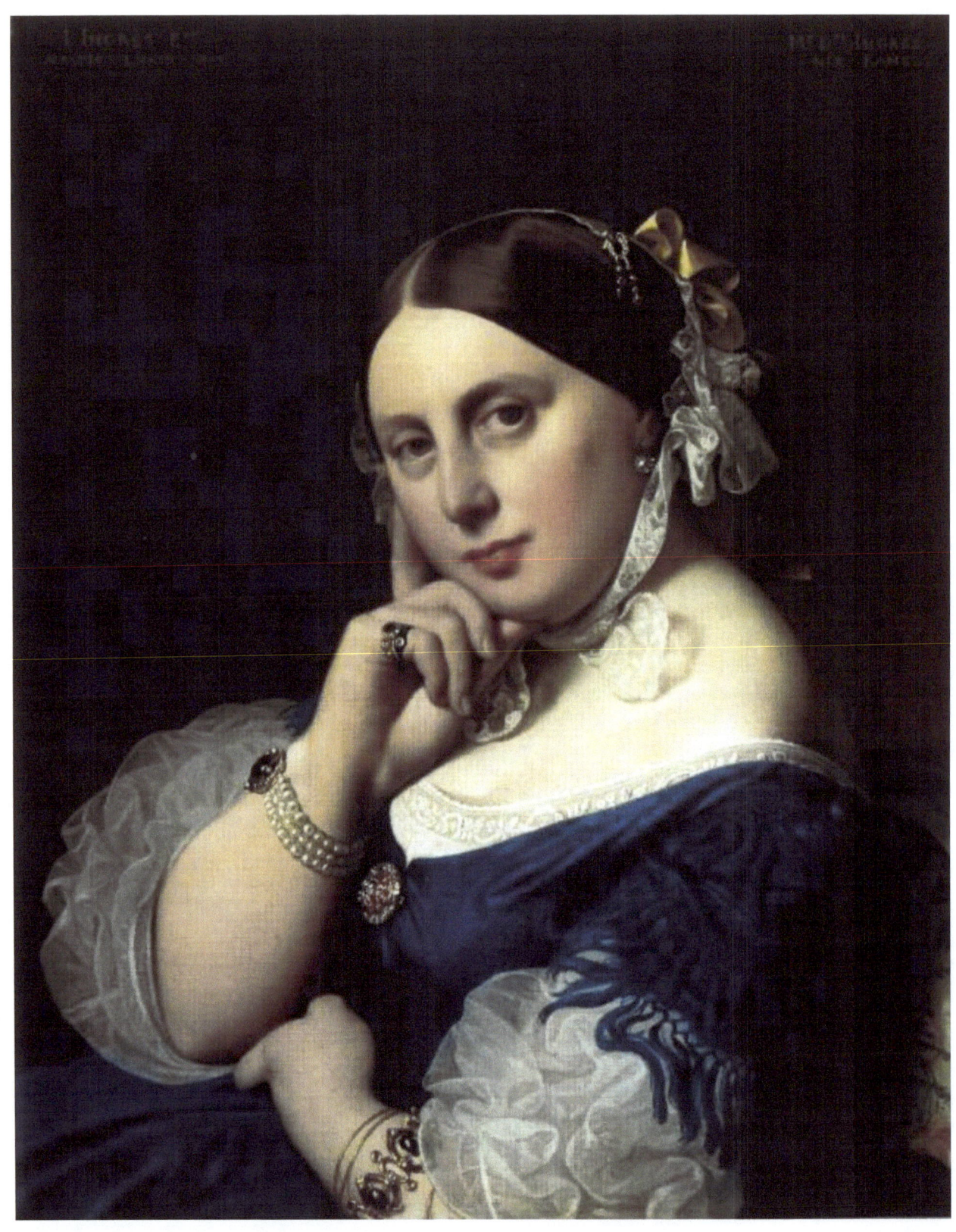

Delphine Ramel, Madame Ingres

1859, oil on canvas

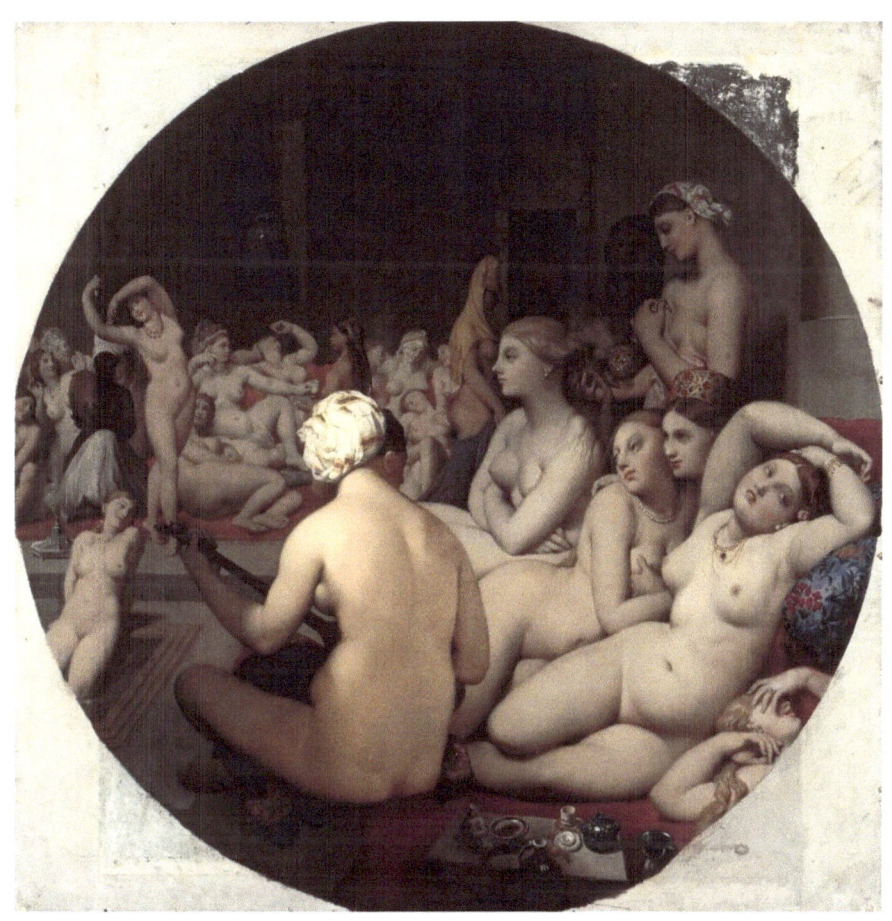

The Turkish Bath

1863, oil on canvas

Ingres derived the idea of these swarming nudes in the interior of a harem from Lady Mary Wortley Montague's letters. She was the wife of the English ambassador to the Sublime Porte; in these two letters she describes baths in the Seraglio, which she was allowed to enter, and Ingres copied extracts from them into his notebook, probably in about 1817.Several of the figures in this canvas have been taken from earlier pictures; others are new. Ingres had not a very ready imagination, and borrowed from both French and English prints of 'turqueries', going back to the eighteenth or even the sixteenth centuries. Copies of these are still to be seen in the archives of his studio in the Musñe de Montauban.This picture has existed in at least two forms. A first sketch, intended for Comte Demidoff, was executed in 1852, but not delivered; it was probably worked on again after this date, and at the end of 1859 it was bought by Prince Napoleon. The appearance of this picture, which at that time was square, is known from a photograph dated 7 October 1859. On the intervention of Princess Clotilde, scandalized by all those nudes, the Prince returned it to Ingres; M. Reiset was entrusted with negotiating its exchange for a portrait of the artist at the age of twenty-four (now in the Musee Conde, Chantilly). Ingres kept the picture for several years, making various changes in it and giving it its final circular form. He signed it in 1862, indicating with pride that it was the work of a man of eighty-two.

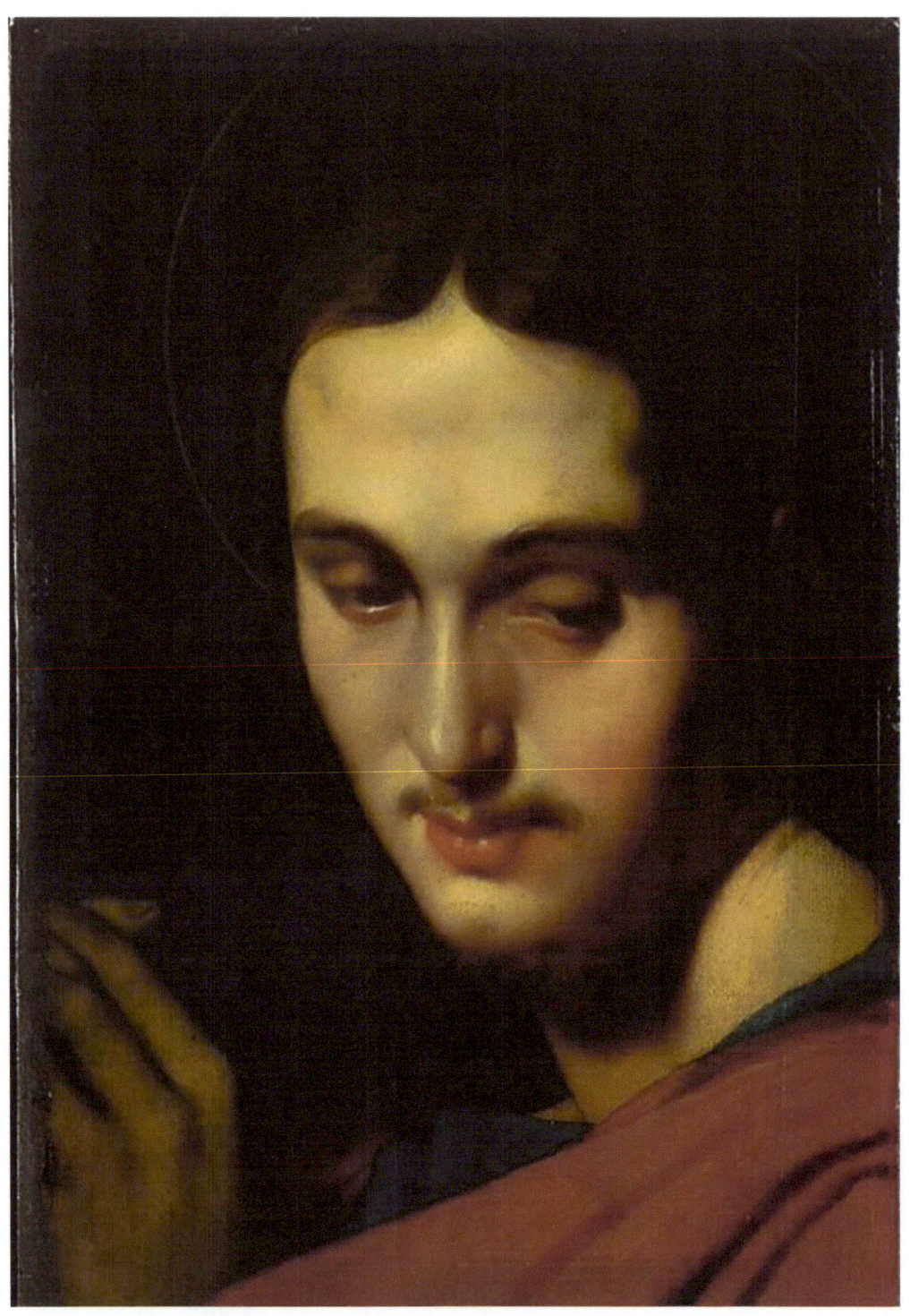

Head of Saint John the Evangelist, oil on canvas

This is a study for an altarpiece, Christ Delivering the Keys to Saint Peter, commissioned in 1817 for Santissima Trinità dei Monti, Rome, and completed in 1820 (now Musée Ingres, Montauban). Ingres based the composition on Raphael's tapestry design of the same theme and developed it in eight oil studies (including this one) and more than seventy drawings. Although the study may date to 1818–20, it is also possible that it was painted or reworked in 1841, and touches may have added as late as 1856.

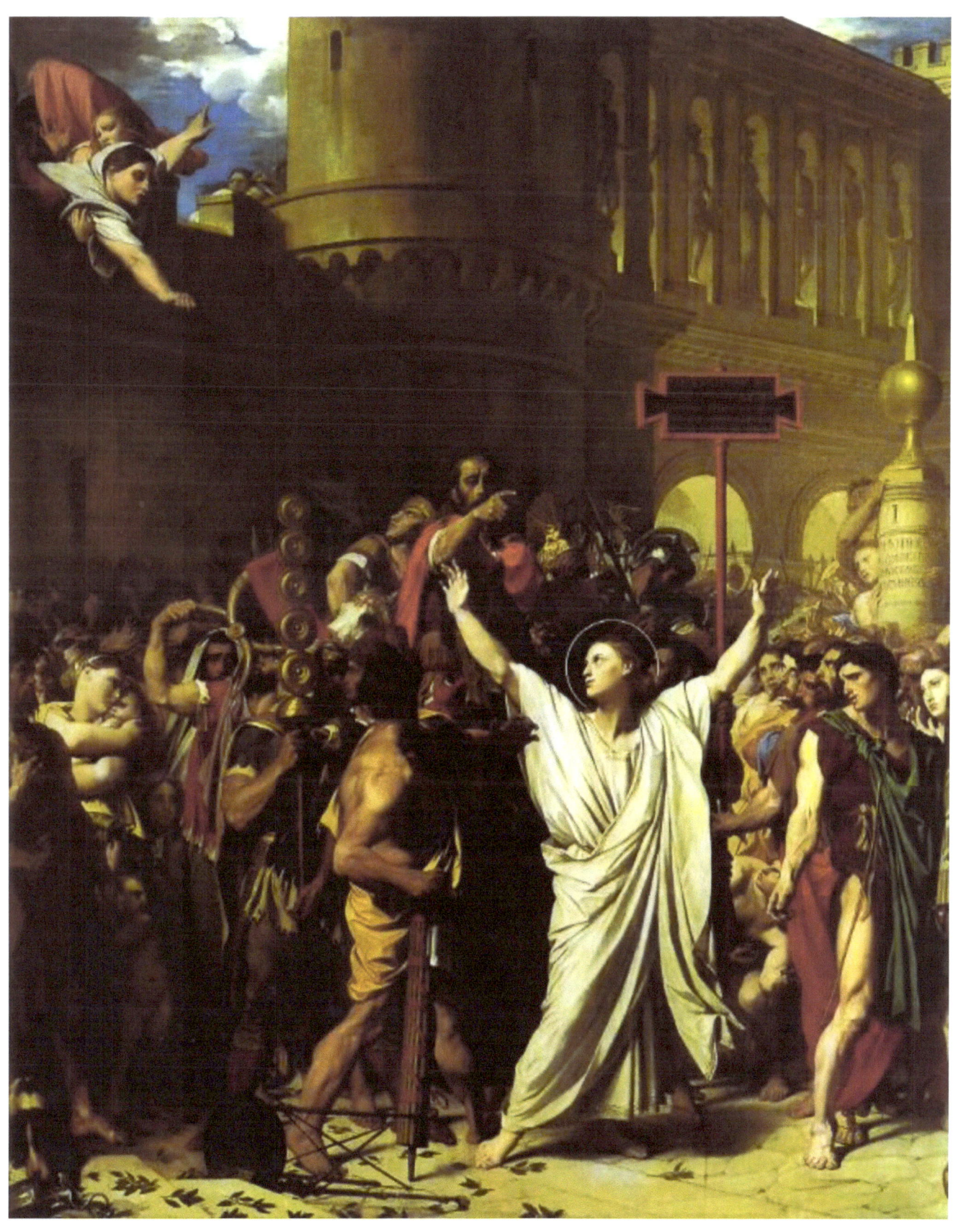

The Martyrdom of St. Symphorian

1834, oil on canvas

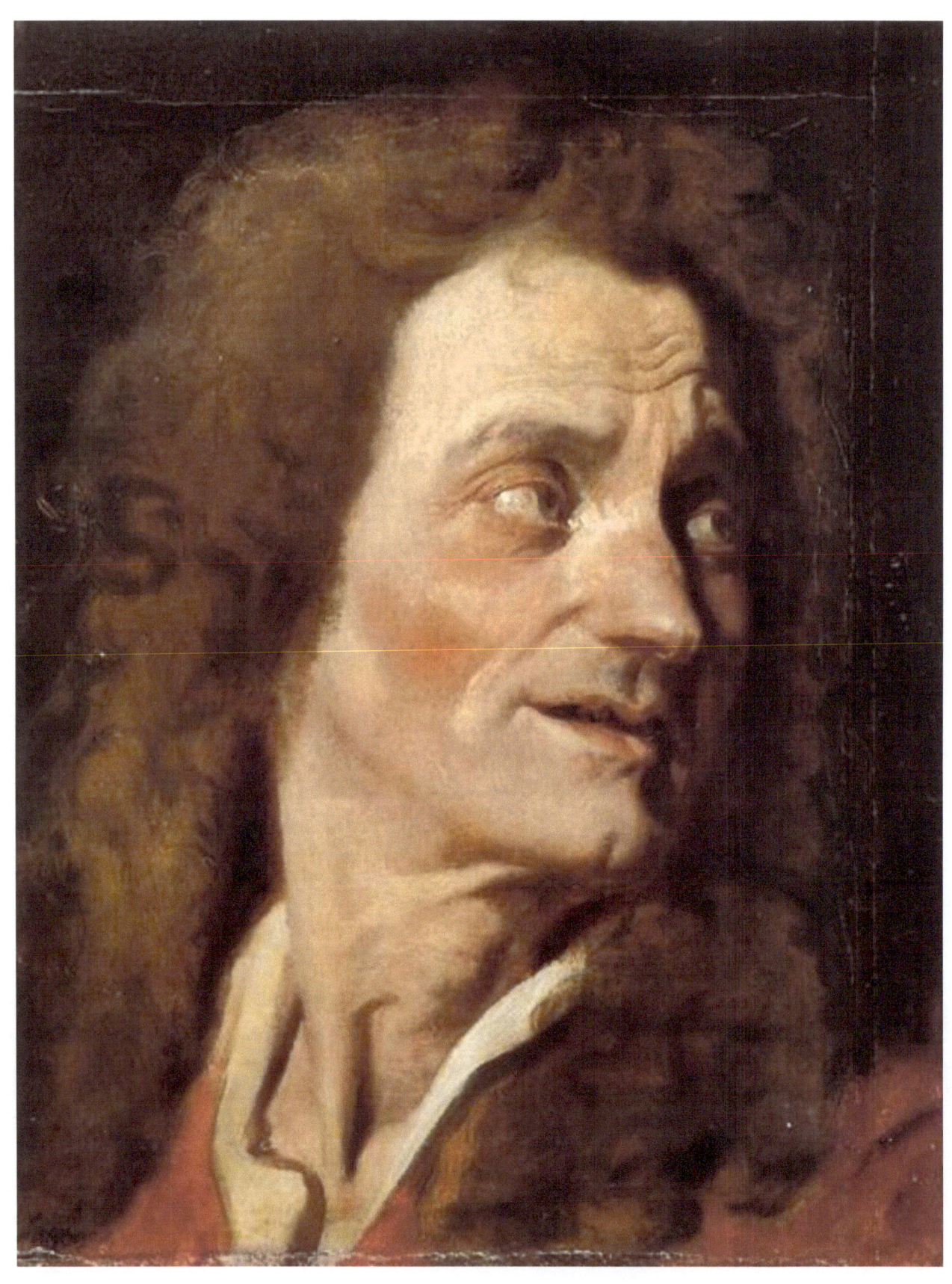

Head of Boileau

1827, oil on canvas

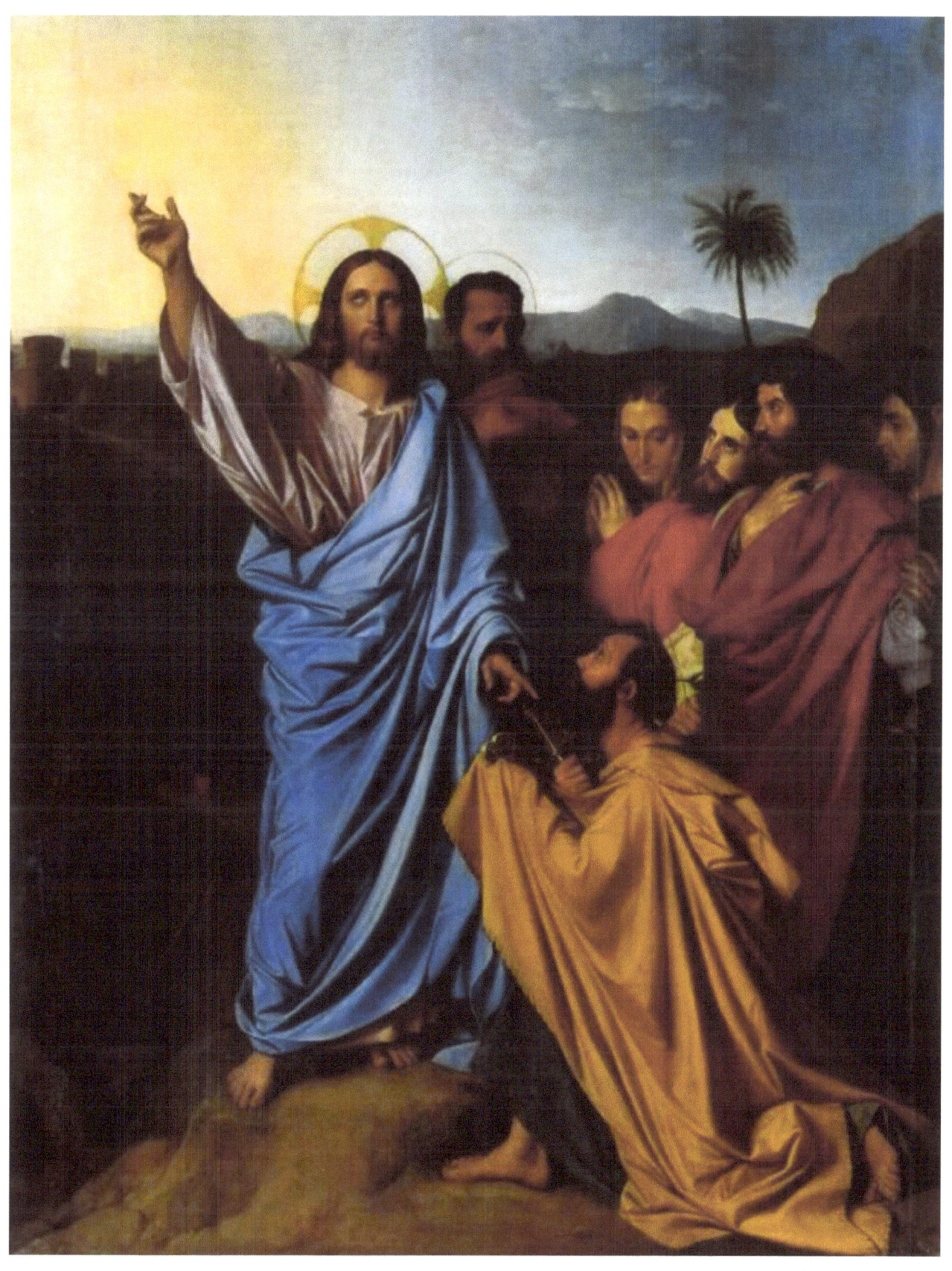

Jesus Returning the Keys to St. Peter

1820, oil on canvas

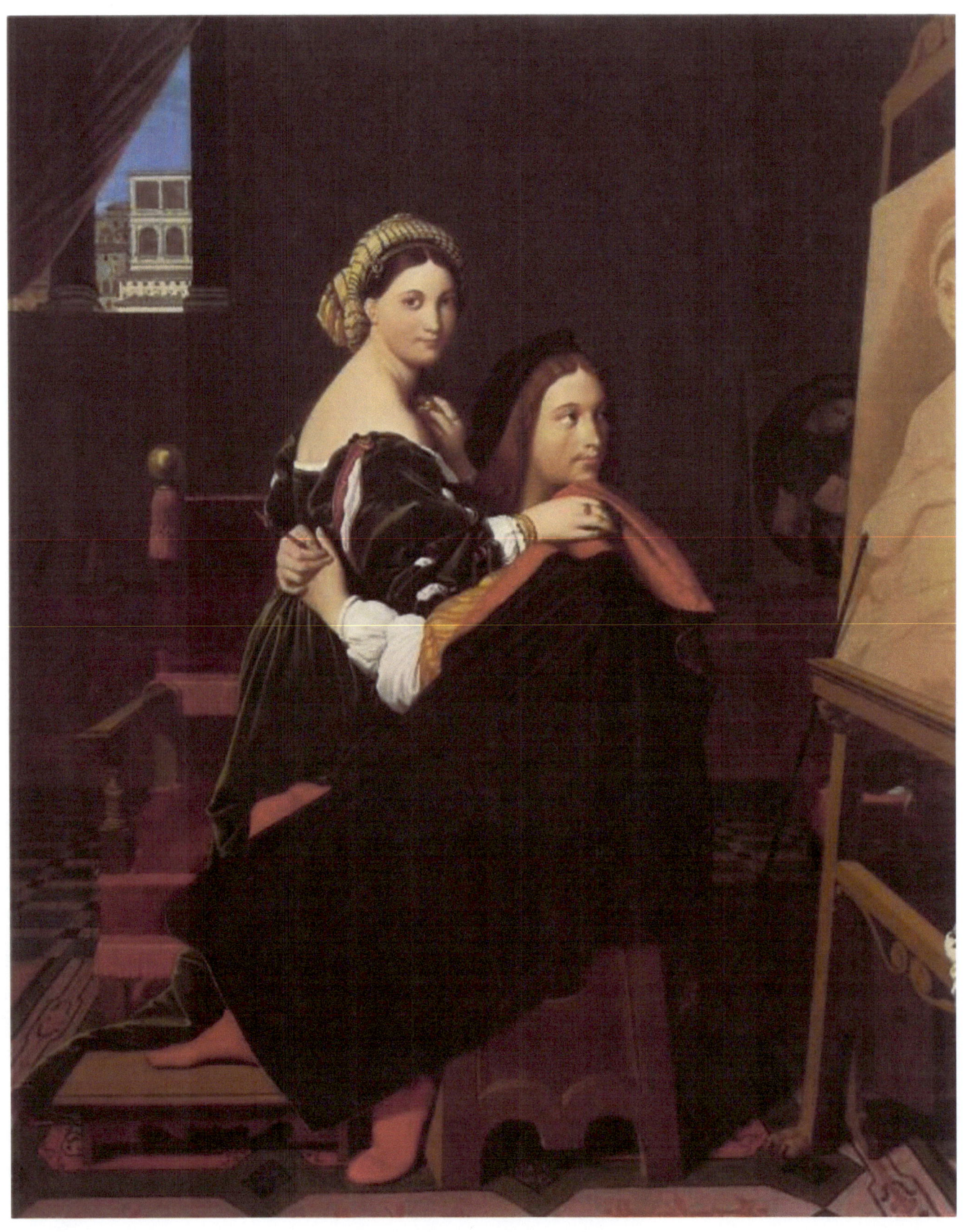

Raphael and the Fornarina

1814, oil on canvas